ORIENTAL RUGS
of the
HAJJI BABAS

DANIEL S. WALKER

ORIENTAL RUGS of the HAJJI BABAS

PUBLISHED BY
THE ASIA SOCIETY AND
HARRY N. ABRAMS, INC.
NEW YORK

IN ASSOCIATION
WITH SOTHEBY'S

Oriental Rugs of the Hajji Babas is the catalogue of an exhibition shown at The Asia Society in the spring of 1982. The exhibition will also be presented at The Textile Museum, Washington, D.C.; the Seattle Art Museum; and the Cincinnati Art Museum.

This project is made possible by a grant from the Andrew W. Mellon Foundation and generous assistance from Sotheby Parke Bernet Inc. and members of the Hajji Baba Club.

Library of Congress Catalog Card Number:
81-71117

International Standard Book Number:
0-8109-1436-0

CONTENTS

PREFACE
and
ACKNOWLEDGMENTS

In making the selection of rugs for this exhibition, we have looked for pieces of the highest quality, but we have also been guided by a number of other considerations. Because the exhibition celebrates the fifty-year history of the Hajji Baba Club, we felt that the rugs chosen should present an accurate picture of the interests and acquisitions of the Club's members. Thus the majority of the pieces included here are nineteenth-century rugs made by village and nomad weavers rather than the classical pieces produced in court workshops in earlier centuries. Because Turkoman rugs have always been especially popular among the members, these are represented in larger numbers than other rugs. We had originally planned to concentrate on unpublished material, but this would have excluded some of the best pieces. Nonetheless we have tried not to borrow rugs that have been recently seen in major exhibitions such as *Turkmen: Tribal Carpets and Traditions* at The Textile Museum in Washington, D.C. We also felt that a broad range of collections should be represented and that there should be a balance between private and institutional lenders. Finally, we have made an effort to include rugs once owned by early Club members, particularly the five founders.

A few remarks about the catalogue entries may be helpful. Unless otherwise indicated, the rugs included here have been lent anonymously from private collections. Measurements of the rugs were made along the central axes to the full extent of warp and weft used together, thus including skirts but excluding fringes. Technical analyses were executed by the author, with the exception of that for no. 50, which was provided by Nobuko Kajitani of The Metropolitan Museum of Art.

I am deeply grateful to the members of the Hajji Baba Club, who have assisted me in every way they could. In particular I would like to mention the contribution of Charles Grant Ellis, who gave me invaluable help in locating and selecting pieces and provided useful information on the older rugs in the exhibition. Olive Olmstead Foster, devoted secretary of the Club, gave me extensive assistance in the preparation of the introductory essay on the Club's history. Her previously published writings were, in fact, principal sources for that essay. My colleagues at the various lending institutions have been exceedingly generous with their time and resources, and I am deeply grateful for their help. Finally, I thank my wife, Barbara Walker, for her support and patience.

DANIEL S. WALKER

On behalf of The Asia Society, I would like to thank the many discerning collectors who have lent us their rugs, helped us to assemble this exhibition, and contributed funds to the project. Hajjis Joseph Reinis, Bruce Westcott, and John McHugh were principally responsible for the negotiations that led to our collaboration with the Hajji Baba Club. Alvin Pearson provided a planning grant which enabled Daniel Walker and Charles Grant Ellis to visit collections of Hajji Baba members and museums throughout the United States. Michael Grogan, assistant vice-president and head of the rug department at Sotheby Parke Bernet Inc., graciously arranged for most of the rugs from private collections to be photographed and stored at Sotheby's until our own storage facilities were ready. The Textile Conservation Workshop in South Salem, New York, was responsible for preparing the private loans for exhibition. We are also grateful to the trustees and staff of the three institutions participating in the tour of the exhibition: The Textile Museum, Washington, D.C., the Seattle Art Museum, and the Cincinnati Art Museum. Donald Goddard provided invaluable editorial assistance, and the staff of Harry N. Abrams, Inc., has been unfailingly helpful in producing this book on a very tight schedule. My own staff has handled their diverse responsibilities with characteristic efficiency and good humor. I am grateful to them all.

ALLEN WARDWELL
Director
Asia Society Gallery

FOREWORD

The word *rug* can have a rather mundane connotation, but when it is combined with another word, a word with which it is most often associated, all sorts of wonderful and unexpected things take place in our minds. The other word is, of course, *Oriental*.

Oriental rugs conjure up childhood fantasies. They are magic carpets. They decorated the walls, floors, doors, and pillows of the places frequented by Ali Baba and all his contemporaries and companions. No part of the Arabia we envisioned as we read the fascinating tales of genies and a thousand and one nights was without its Oriental weavings somewhere in the background.

The romance, mystery, and exoticism with which Oriental rugs were originally associated all remain with them, no matter how "grown up" the curator, collector, or connoisseur might be. Reading through the literature on the subject, one is struck by the youthful enthusiasm and passionate commitment the authors almost invariably reveal. In *The Oriental Carpet* (New York: Abrams, 1981), P. R. J. Ford writes with firsthand knowledge of the reasons why Oriental rugs enchant their admirers (p. 28): "For the Western buyer. . . many Oriental carpets represent more than the artistic expression of a single individual: they embody the experience of a whole people, they are an expression of the achievements and sufferings of a different cultural tradition and, beyond that, of the aspirations of the human spirit. The desert nomad, struggling to create out of sheep's wool and goat hair the flowers in the garden that he can never have, speaks to us through his carpet."

Collectors, particularly those of earlier generations, may have found that the act of acquiring a carpet provided some of the most fascinating, exasperating, and ultimately satisfying moments of their lives. While the acquisition of any work of art involves an interesting story, the Westerner who has bought a rug in a Middle Eastern bazaar, with all the noise, the cups of coffee, the backroom techniques, and the intense bargaining, has had an adventure. He has been intimately involved in a very different world from that of the private dealer or elegant auction house. The carpet thus won represents for him an unusual experience, a tale, and even—if the rug merchant was clever enough—a bargain.

The more common incentives for art appreciation are there as well. The objects themselves are beautiful. They enhance the homes and prestige of their owners in the West much as they did in the countries of their origin. They stimulate intense discussion concerning matters of provenance and technique. They also provide fine material for exhibitions such as this one.

The works included here are among the best of their kind and show many of the great weaving styles and expressions of the Asian "rug belt." Each piece represents the culmination of a long conservative tradition and is a marvel of craftsmanship. This exhibition is not, however, merely another survey of distinguished examples of the rug-maker's art. By celebrating the fiftieth anniversary of the Hajji Baba Club, America's prime rug-collecting society, the exhibition provides an important chapter in the history of the appreciation and collection of rugs in this country. Every one of the rugs shown here from a private collection is owned by a Hajji member, and those that come from museum collections were donated by Hajjis and are among the institutions' treasures. As is immediately evident from Daniel Walker's introduction, the Hajji Baba Club is no ordinary collectors' society. Its members were and are opinionated, enthusiastic, knowledgeable, and obsessed. They are private collectors, museum curators, and scholars who have made an incalculable contribution to our understanding of this Asian art.

Although the last half century has seen extraordinary growth in the appreciation and connoisseurship of Oriental rugs, it represents only the latest phase in a long history of interest on the part of the West. By the beginning of the fourteenth century certain types of Oriental rugs were already beginning to appear on the European continent. Although no documented examples are known to have survived from this period, depictions of rugs can be found in some Italian panel paintings and frescoes by such fourteenth-century masters as Giotto and Simone Martini. These rugs seem to have come from Turkey, and are thought to have been made at Konya and other neighboring weaving centers such as Beyshehir. Undoubtedly the proximity of Turkish ports to the Mediterranean shipping lanes and to Venice was an important factor in bringing these weavings to the attention of Europeans.

During the fourteenth and fifteenth centuries, most probably only Turkish rugs were collected in Europe. When the Portuguese opened trading routes around the Cape of Good Hope in the sixteenth century, the crafts of Persia, Afghanistan, and Turkoman Anatolia soon became avidly sought after, and different varieties of Oriental carpets appear with increasing regularity in both the religious and secular paintings of Italy, Spain, and the Low Countries from this time until the late eighteenth century. They are shown covering tables, draped over balconies, placed on the floor before enthroned madonnas, or even decorating altars. Although the so-called Lotto and Holbein carpets are the most famous of these (both are, incidentally, Ushaks of Anatolian Turkoman provenance), Oriental carpets appear in the works of other artists such as Vermeer, Breughel, van Eyck, Memling, Velázquez, Rubens, and Van Dyck. From these documents, it is evident that these rugs were highly regarded by affluent European collectors of the time.

During the late sixteenth and the seventeenth century, emissaries were also sent from Europe to the Persian courts of Shah 'Abbas and his Safavid successors. They returned with some of the great carpets that are now preserved in European royal collections. All the rugs that came to the Continent during this period were what we now call classical rugs, that is, rugs that were made under royal patronage. Interest in the utilitarian weavings of the nomad and village people of Asia Minor had not yet surfaced. Nor were rugs from India and China available or sought after until later times.

During the late eighteenth century, European preferences for carpets shifted to works that were made on the Continent itself, particularly in France. Rugs from the Aubusson and Savonnerie workshops were especially popular. This change in taste coincided with the decline in the manufacture of classical carpets in Persia and Turkey. Royal patronage had ceased, owing to such political events as the fall of the Safavid Dynasty, and with the weakening of European interest, commercial production fell off as well.

None of this had any effect on the production of rugs by the nomad and village peoples, who used these textiles for a much wider variety of purposes than simply as floor coverings. As large hangings and smaller woven pieces known as tent bands, they decorated walls. They surrounded the doors of tent entrances, covered pillows and pieces of furniture, were made into bags for storage and transportation of goods and belongings, and were used as trappings, saddle covers, and blankets for horses and camels alike. They served as belts, provided warmth and decoration in the form of coverlets, and had an important religious significance as prayer rugs. Here too rugs were also prestige items that displayed wealth and status, and in the village bazaars they represented pieces of considerable commercial value. Weavings of this nature truly reflect the lives of the people who used them.

These textiles were virtually ignored in the West until the latter part of the nineteenth century. Then, quite suddenly, a demand for less expensive and more functional carpets emerged, and a thriving trade in the more humble products of the villages of Asia Minor was established. Merchants scoured previously neglected bazaars and sought weavings from the very homes in which they were still being used, and it was not long before these village people began to make rugs solely for commercial purposes. Under the guidance of opportunistic merchants, who often supplied raw materials and already conceived designs to artisans, rug-weaving workshops were formed. The weavers were often children, who were given minimal wages for long hours of labor and whose small and nimble fingers could work with speed and efficiency. The products of these "factories" appeared throughout Europe and America during the late nineteenth and early twentieth centuries. Although they lack the fresh creativity of the legitimate utilitarian weavings of Asia Minor whose designs were in the minds of their creators, they probably were what most people of the time knew to be "Oriental rugs."

The resurgence of interest in Oriental carpets provided the catalyst for the formation in 1932 of the Hajji Baba Club. Its members did not, of course, search out the mass-produced rugs mentioned above. Instead they enthusiastically collected, studied, and fought over the true nomad and peasant weavings, which were much more readily available than the costly, more luxurious classical carpets made under court patronage. Although some early members of the Club did collect classical carpets, the predominant interest of the membership has always been the spontaneous village creations. It is therefore those which have been chosen for exhibition here. Price, availability, and beauty have been among the factors governing this predilection. It is also true that these pieces are somewhat more practical to live with and enjoy, owing to their comparatively small scale.

This brings us to a brief examination of The Asia Society's inadequate involvement with this field during its own twenty-two-year history. It might seem surprising that this is only the third rug exhibition to have been shown in our galleries, and only the second to have been organized here. Back in 1961, Maurice Dimand (then, as today, a Hajji) put together his *Peasant and Nomad Rugs of Asia*. It was the seventh exhibition to be held at the old Asia House Gallery, and it served to bring wider public recognition to these fascinating works at an early period in the history of The Asia Society. This was followed, much later, by another "nomad and peasant" exhibition: *From the Bosporus to Samarkand,* which was organized by the Textile Museum in Washington, D.C., in 1972. Unfortunately, this was too large an exhibition to fit into the two small rooms that served the gallery, and some rugs simply could not be shown, while others adorned hallways and other areas that were not part of the gallery itself. Therein is the problem. Most rug exhibitions are simply too large for our limited spaces, and although we acknowledge that rug weaving is one of Asia's preeminent arts, we also recognize the fact that we have not done it justice.

For this reason, this event is a particularly happy one for The Asia Society. The carpets collected by the Hajjis fit as well into the intimate space of our gallery as they do into their owners' homes. At the same time we are able to provide detailed information about one of the great expressions of Asia and to honor a group of enthusiasts who have enhanced our appreciation and knowledge of a subject they have loved.

ALLEN WARDWELL

THE HAJJI BABA CLUB
1932-1982

The appreciation of Oriental rugs in the United States has fluctuated dramatically. Incredible peaks of enthusiasm during the first three decades of this century followed the earliest major European studies and exhibitions of rugs. Then came thirty years of general lack of interest, affecting all but a few lonely souls, and finally twenty years of renewed fervor.

The two periods of keen interest were, and are, very different in nature. In the early years of American rug collecting, a relatively small number of men purchased for large sums of money rugs dating primarily from the classical phase of rug production, the sixteenth and seventeenth centuries. Typical of this group of collectors was Senator William A. Clark of Montana, whose rugs now belong to the Corcoran Gallery of Art in Washington, D.C. Early in this century, Senator Clark paid $100,000 at auction for a single Indo-Persian carpet.

By contrast, the recent phase has involved increasing numbers of collectors of relatively modest means, and attention has turned to the tribal and village weavings. Previously spurned by all the great collectors except James F. Ballard, tribal and village rugs are now seen to illustrate the continuity of the age-old rug-weaving traditions, whereas the rugs of the classical period, which have almost disappeared from the marketplace, are considered to symbolize a unique moment when court patronage and commercial interests stimulated the production of works of great luxury and trade pieces alien to those traditions.

The rapid growth of rug collecting in recent decades and the proliferation of rug clubs throughout the United States can be attributed, in large part, to the influence of the Hajji Baba Club, the oldest and most prestigious American rug club. It is ironic that the Club, which celebrates its fiftieth anniversary in 1982, was founded at a time when general interest in Oriental rugs had reached a new low.

The birth of the Hajji Baba Club in 1932 was a direct result of the publication a year earlier of *Oriental Rugs and Carpets* by Arthur Urbane Dilley, the noted rug dealer, authority, and lecturer. But the Great Depression had put an abrupt halt to the formation of major rug collections, and 1931 was clearly the wrong time to interest the general public in a field of luxury collectibles. In spite of enthusiastic reviews in *The New York Times Book Review* and *The Times Literary Supplement*, Dilley's book sold poorly. After two years, out of an edition of 5,000 copies, fewer than 1,000 had been sold.

In spite of the book's financial failure, Dilley apparently considered this publication the climax of his career. He took immense pride in it particularly because, as he later said in one of his numerous papers, "No rug book even the least worthy of respect had suffered a similar calamity. Yet, strangely, none achieved a comparable success—the creation of a club of men and eventually women of rare culture."

Dilley's book, despite its limited distribution, did have a profound impact on a number of individuals. Roy Winton, managing director of the

Arthur Urbane Dilley

Amateur Cinema League, an international organization of home motion picture makers, and Arthur Gale, editor of the magazine *Movie Makers*, had developed their enthusiasm for Oriental rugs while furnishing the apartment they shared in New York City. When *Oriental Rugs and Carpets* appeared, they looked up Dilley to congratulate him and immediately struck up a friendship.

To this small group was added Anton Lau, a consulting engineer who was an acquaintance of Dilley's, and Arthur Arwine, a collector of Turkoman rugs. Dilley did not know Arwine, but had seen photographs of his New York apartment at One Sheridan Square, where Arwine had arranged some of his rugs to give his home the look of a Turkoman dwelling, a spirited but impossible quest in square rooms with furniture, fireplaces, and high ceilings. It was not long before these five men began to gather at Arwine's apartment to share their interest in rugs. Meetings continued early in 1932, either at Arwine's or at Winton and Gale's, and the idea of forming a club must have come up at that time.

The organizational meeting of the Hajji Baba Club was held at the home of Tony Lau, in Bloomfield, New Jersey, on July 9, 1932. Present were the five founders—Lau, Arthur Arwine, Arthur Urbane Dilley, Arthur Gale, and Roy Winton. Dilley was elected president of the new club, named at first The Oriental Rug Club of New York but then renamed the Hajji Baba Club, at Dilley's suggestion. The minutes of that meeting note that "the speech of acceptance by the President lasted for a period of sixty-two minutes

and was received with loud applause and great acclaim; it required the unremitting efforts of the full membership which constituted itself Sergeant-at-Arms-at-Large to restore order." Winton must have played a key role in the organizational process because he was extended a vote of thanks by the Club for his efforts.

The name selected for the Club belonged to a fictional Persian rogue and con man, the subject of an amusing novel of 1824 by James Morier, an English diplomat. Hajji Baba, the son of a barber of Isfahan, finds himself involved in one desperate or comical fix after another, which he solves by guile, charm, or self-promotion. He changes careers constantly, rising from lowly water-carrier to chief secretary to the ambassador of England. Yet in spite of his methods of operation, Hajji Baba seems a thoroughly likeable character, no doubt because he is surrounded by scoundrels far more devilish and corrupt than he. Dilley felt that Hajji Baba was the Club's natural patron saint because "he was a rogue who never paid more than ten cents on the dollar," a quality that particularly endeared him to Depression-era collectors.

It was in the spirit of Hajji Baba that a Club motto was created: "In the fine arts, including folly, some find the release and peace, the reward and joy, that others obtain from religion." But it was in a more serious and generous spirit that the early members stated the purpose of the Club in their new constitution: "The object of the Club shall be to promote the knowledge and appreciation of Oriental rugs as an art and to furnish a medium of association for students and collectors of

Arthur Arwine's apartment at One Sheridan Square, New York City. The rug on the fireplace mantel is no. 39 in this selection.

such rugs. As a means of accomplishing this object, the Club may hold meetings, sponsor lectures and exhibitions, conduct tours to great collections, publish books and papers and, in general, engage in any activity which will contribute to the accomplishment of its object."

Dilley wrote with particular fondness, in a manuscript entitled "Group Portrait of Club Founders and the Times in Which They Lived," of the other four founding members: "Pleasant memories are portraits one would wish never to forget: Arwine's splendid collection of Turkoman rugs which to him filled the void of wife and child, . . . Lau collecting rug data, both fact and fancy, scrap-book fashion, as if to compile an encyclopedia. The eagerness of Winton and Gale to solve the thousand riddles of nomenclature, as if knowing a name determined the difference between knowledge and ignorance, appreciation and indifference. They knew it to be merely the first step. Finally, long before my acquaintance with these splendid men, my own inconquerable will to write my own version of rugs from the notes of many lectures, my office door locked against business intrusion. No mutual admiration society ever existed that eclipsed the fervor of this one."

These four all played vital roles in the early days of the Club, to be sure, but it was really Arthur Dilley himself who provided the impetus to launch the Club and to develop such a full program of activities. Dilley remained president for the first twelve years of the Club's existence. He was described at the age of sixty-seven in Richard

15

O. Boyer's 1939 profile for *The New Yorker* as "a tall, prim man with ruddy, severe features. He has a booming, hearty voice, with which he strives to conceal a timidity which, he says, he has never quite been able to overcome. He wears gray spats, a green signet ring, pince-nez, and usually carries a tightly rolled umbrella. He will remove his hat in the most closely packed elevator if a woman is present. He takes a good deal of pleasure in regarding himself as a gentleman of the old school."

Educated at Harvard, and subsequently an English Master at the Taft School until he turned to rug dealing professionally, Dilley remained thoughout his life something of an aesthete. His deep interest in rugs, furniture, trees, and birds was complemented by a love of English literature which seemed to touch everything he did. In spite of the considerable rug lore contained in his *Oriental Rugs and Carpets*, Dilley always looked upon this work as a literary achievement, citing with great pride the textbook on expository writing which quoted from his book and put his name in an index that included Lamb and Dickens.

Dilley's aristocratic bearing and elegance made him something of an anomaly in the marketplace. Witnessing an incomprehensible conversation between Armenian dealers, he would freeze "into a monument of Anglo-Saxon suspicion," as Boyer put it. Dilley never considered himself a salesman at all, taking great pains to bring new dignity to his chosen profession. When a publisher observed that rugs were rugs, with only minor differences, and wondered what service Dilley provided, he received this frosty reply, extensively shortened here: " 'I'm thinking how alike they are,' I explained, 'alike as Coleridge's *Kubla Khan* and Gibbon's *Decline and Fall*. Only a negligible difference separates a poet constructing a palace and a historian tearing one down. Alike as Marlowe's *Tamburlaine the Great* and Lew Wallace's *Prince of India*, who, had they been harnessed to any old chariot, could have beaten Kim and Omar Khayyám pulling a rubber-tired sulky. Surely to clarify such a mélange is to render a service.' "

Arthur Urbane Dilley was a successful dealer who maintained high principles and was consulted by such collectors as James Ballard and C. F. Williams. Perhaps because of his distaste for the commercial aspects of his work, Dilley seemed to take great pleasure in lecturing, where he could spread the gospel without actually resorting to selling. He lectured a great deal, giving fifty-seven lectures in two years in New England early in his career, and as many as two lectures a day for three weeks in the 1920s when he traveled with Ballard's collection. But Dilley seemed to take the greatest satisfaction, particularly in his later years, in the club he had helped to found. When he died in 1959, all rights to *Oriental Rugs and Carpets*, which had just been published in a second edition revised by Maurice Dimand, were left to the Hajji Baba Club.

Membership in the Club, which was achieved by personal acquaintance or introduction, grew gradually in these first years. Two new members were accepted in 1933. Harold Olivet was so impressed by an early book of Dilley's which he found in a library that he called him and was

Joseph V. McMullan

steered to the recently published 1931 book. Olivet started attending meetings and soon was a member.

The other 1933 addition to the roster, Joseph McMullan, made a much brasher entrance. Joe, as he was known to all, developed his interest in Oriental rugs after buying a bad one with poor wool and painted colors. As he related in his first paper for the Club, investigation led him to rug books and a few more purchases. One day in B. Altman's, he saw two rug fragments that appealed to him. He returned on another occasion, found that one had been sold, purchased the second one, and then tracked down the buyer of the first fragment. Arthur Gale recalled that he and Roy Winton were having dinner with Winton's parents on 40th Street when Joe McMullan appeared and asked in his very direct way, "Is this the Winton that bought the Transylvanian rug fragment?" Having proven his mettle as a Hajji by buying such a worthwhile piece, Joe was invited to join the group.

Joseph McMullan's contributions to the Club over the many years of his membership were enormous. He gave papers, he brought to meetings for good-natured discussions some of his recent acquisitions, which were numerous, and he succeeded Dilley as the second president of the Club, from 1944 to 1946. He became well known beyond the immediate circle of the Club through his lecturing and through various exhibitions of his rugs, first at the Fogg Art Museum at Harvard in 1949 and 1954, subsequently in Lahore and Karachi under the sponsorship of the State Depart-

ment in 1958, and finally at the Metropolitan Museum of Art in New York in 1970 and at the Hayward Gallery in London in 1972. Various catalogues accompanied these exhibitions, but the grand production was his *Islamic Rugs*, published in 1965, which has always been highly regarded for its superlative color plates and for the personal and perceptive commentary provided by McMullan.

A New Yorker by birth, McMullan was a self-taught engineer and construction man who rose to the vice-presidency of the Naylor Pipe Company of Chicago, a firm whose greatest success was Joe's design of the so-called invasion pipe, an easily assembled portable pipeline used extensively during World War II in North Africa. His collection was particularly strong in the village rugs of Anatolia, rugs whose beauty he was known for discovering. Whether or not the McMullan rug collection was the greatest ever assembled, as has been suggested, it certainly contained extraordinary material.

Joe and his wife, Connie, put on every activity with which they were involved the stamps of their very individual, irrepressible personalities. Arthur Jenkins, currently president of the Board of Trustees of the Textile Museum in Washington, D.C., and long-time Hajji, recalls a visit he and Joe once made to the St. Louis Art Museum to view the Ballard rugs. In the process of rooting around in storage, they unearthed a fine Star Ushak from a pile of far lesser weavings. Shocked that the museum did not know what it had, Joe brought the rug to the attention of the museum administration, and the Sunday newspapers mentioned it. When McMullan and Jenkins appeared at the museum on Sunday morning, a line of visitors eager to see the new discovery had already formed. Since the rug had not been put on display, and since no one from the curatorial staff was present, the two visitors cajoled the guards into unlocking the storeroom. They brought out the rug, set up rope barriers, opened several copies of the catalogue of the museum's rugs to the appropriate page, gave the guards a crash training course, and let the public in.

In spite of her long association with the Hajji Baba Club, Connie McMullan did not become a member of the Club until 1957, the first year women were elected to membership. Prior to that year, women's involvement in Club activities had been restricted to picnics and special outings. The original constitution specified male members only, since the writers of the constitution, Winton and Lau, felt that women lacked the proper attitude toward Oriental rugs, buying them merely for reasons of utility.

The year after Olivet and McMullan joined the ranks in 1933, several new members were elected, including Maurice Dimand, Walter Smith, Parsons Todd, Theron Damon, and Fred Kramer. Dimand, curator emeritus of Islamic art at the Metropolitan Museum of Art, has made many contributions to rug scholarship and has served the Club as president for a total of ten years on four different occasions between 1948 and 1971. Parsons Todd was an industrialist, head of a mining company in New York, twice mayor of Morristown, New Jersey, and Club secretary from 1945 to 1964. Theron Damon of Worcester, Massachusetts, had lived in Turkey for twenty-five years while connected with Roberts College, and Fred Kramer was an architect. A number of early members became acquainted at a W.P.A.-sponsored adult-education course on Oriental rugs taught in Greenwich Village in the mid-1930s by Krikor Krikorian. Harold Olivet and Joseph McMullan both attended, and there they met future members Alveda and Alvin Pearson, Newton Foster, Amos Thacher, and Ovid Whelchel. Al Pearson, the retired president of The Lehman Corporation, has served stints both as treasurer and as president of the Club. Newton Foster, a retired engineer formerly with Congoleum Industries, was Club treasurer from 1948 to 1980 and president in 1976–77, while his wife, Olive, retired director of public relations for Fairleigh Dickinson University, continues to serve as Club secretary, a post she has held since 1971. Amos Thacher, a telephone company executive, was Club secretary from 1935 to 1940. Ovid Whelchel, an insurance company lawyer, was Club librarian and compiled a survey of rugs depicted in famous paintings.

Other members from the early days include the architect Julian Levi, Dr. Alva Peckham, Oliver Brantley, president of the Careful Carpet Cleaning Company, and John Shapley, professor of art and architecture at Catholic University, Washington, D.C., and the University of Baghdad. Jerome Straka, retired president of Chesebrough-Pond's, has been active in the Club since 1940 and

McMullan   Thacher   Peckham   10 Members of the
Olivet   Dilley   Gale   Hajji Baba Club
Footer   Brantley   Spring 1940
Levi   Straka

Hajji Baba Club meeting at the Harvard Club, New York City, in 1940. Left to right: Hajjis McMullan, Olivet, Foster, Levi, Thacher, Dilley, Brantley, Straka, Peckham, and Gale.

has served as its president twice and as its secretary from 1940 to 1945. Harry Weaver, who had been personal secretary to Theodore Roosevelt before working for most of his career at Consolidated Edison, was another early member.

Over the years, many members' first experience with the Hajji Baba Club seemed to revolve around Joe McMullan. Charles Grant Ellis was invited to a meeting because of a letter he wrote to McMullan in 1949 about the rugs he had recently seen at the Fogg Art Museum. H. McCoy Jones was introduced to McMullan in the early 1950s by a bookseller because he was buying the right rug books. At about the same time Arthur Jenkins was first invited to a Hajji meeting by a dealer at whose establishment the meeting was to take place. Jenkins had under his arm a small Turkoman bag

face which obviously impressed the dealer. That evening at the meeting, apparently at Joe McMullan's instigation, the dealer quietly offered to buy the piece from Jenkins. Jenkins proved that he was Hajji material by turning him down cold.

It is worth knowing something of these early members because it was they who set the tone for the years to come. They established the values of the Club, as well as the range of its activities. Quite obviously, it is not possible to review here the entire roster of Club members who have contributed so generously over the years. Members have come and still come from many professional ranks—doctors, lawyers, professors, engineers, architects, publishers, and museum people, among others. The July 1981 membership roster lists 78 resident members from the New York area

19

and 41 nonresident members from all over the United States and a number of foreign countries.

Traditionally, meetings have often involved papers given by members or guest speakers on various topics, as well as occasional examinations and discussions of rugs brought in for the occasion—"bought, borrowed, or swindled," as Olivet put it. The Hajji Babas were discovered by *The New Yorker*, and a description of one meeting was provided in "The Talk of the Town" on February 25, 1939:

"The Hajji Baba Club!" you will no doubt exclaim upon learning that there is in the city an organization so named. "What on earth is that?" Well, it's a club of Oriental-rug enthusiasts, thirty-five of them. Most of the members have only an amateur interest, though the president, Arthur Urbane Dilley, is a professional dealer. The Hajji Babas make pilgrimages from time to time to museums and private houses where noteworthy Oriental rugs are to be found. Their scholarship is well enough known to collectors to gain them access to any collection they may want to see. Sometimes they go far afield; they have been to Philadelphia, to see the Widener collection; to Wilmington, to see Henry du Pont's; and to Washington, to see George Myers'.

A while ago we went to a Hajji Baba dinner at the Harvard Club. After an afternoon of rug-gazing, the members always dine together, and as six of them are Harvard men, the Harvard Club is a natural gathering place. That afternoon they had been up to the Metropolitan Museum and brought back with them Dr. Maurice Dimand, the Curator of Oriental Rugs. They were all sitting in the lounge with their chairs drawn up in a circle, *sipping Martinis and occasionally flopping down to examine a small collection of rugs in the centre of the circle. It's the custom for members to bring recent acquisitions for the rest to admire.*

At dinner we sat beside Colonel Roy Winton, head of the Amateur Cinema League and a keen rug man, who told us about Hajji Baba's origin.

After dinner the club heard the report of Mr. Winton, who had seen some of the rugs in Mr. Hearst's Bronx warehouse and thought they might be worth a visit. Then Mr. Joseph McMullan, an iron-pipe salesman by profession, produced a batch of small Turkoman rugs and discussed them learnedly in a jargon we didn't understand. "Look at the floral patterns in the pants and skirt of this thing," he said. "It will stand up against any big-league stuff." Mr. Amos Thacher, secretary of the club and a Telephone Company executive, was excited. "May I take it home with me?" he asked. Several of the Hajji Babas, we noticed, kept busy during the discussion by repairing rugs with a needle and yarn. The meeting closed with a discussion of what they had seen at the Met that afternoon, Mr. McMullan remarking, "The whole story of the garden carpet will have to be rewritten in the light of what we saw." On the way out we noticed several Hajjis sneering, in a well-bred way, at the anilin-bright piling on the floor of the Harvard Club's lobby.

Later that year, Richard O. Boyer, in his *New Yorker* profile of Arthur Dilley, gave his impression of a Hajji Baba meeting:

The Hajji Babas have a game they enjoy immensely. A rug is spread out before them, perhaps in the home of a

20

collector, the store of a dealer, or even in a museum. If it is a fine one, the Hajji Babas sink to their knees and with whimpers of delight, little mewing sounds of pleasure, they will crawl over it. Some of them whip out magnifying glasses, get down on all fours, and talk to themselves, their eyes pressed close to the rug. Mr. Dilley is usually smoking a pipe, and while his colleagues swarm over the rug in an ecstasy of inquiry, he merely glances at it or feels it between his thumb and forefinger.

"Well," Mr. Dilley said recently at one of the Club's sessions, which was held in a dealer's showroom, "what have we here? Is it Chinese? Persian? Caucasian?" The boldest of spirits in the deductive trials are Joseph V. McMullan, a salesman of pipe; Amos B. Thacher, an executive in the Telephone Company; and Oliver W. Brantley, president of the Careful Carpet Cleaning Company.

"That's a Ladik," McMullan said. "I can tell by its border." Thacher had crawled partly under the rug so he could see its back without inconveniencing those examining its pattern. "Extraordinary! Extraordinary! Wool from a fat-tailed sheep in the spring of the year," he muttered from beneath. "From the under side of the neck, I'd say." Mr. Thacher contorted himself to get more light, so that he could use his magnifying glass.

"It's a Kashan," another member said, "because all Kashans have blue webs." This was evidently a joke, for there was a burst of laughter, and the jester said it again.

"Gentlemen, you're not thinking," said Mr. Dilley professorially. "What is the significance of this pattern?" he asked, touching a part of the design that rested on Mr. Thacher's head. "There's the same item here"— he pointed—"with a variation in the internal pattern.

Shows the weaver was thinking all the time."

"Well, fellows," McMullan said, "I'll stick my neck out and say it's Karabagh and mean it."

Mr. Thacher stuck his neck out and asked, "Just for the sake of argument, will someone tell us why it isn't a Kurd? The warps are of a type of wool perfectly consistent with that theory, and so is the brilliance of the coloring."

"That doesn't hurt my Karabagh theory," McMullan said.

"Gentlemen," said Mr. Dilley, "you're not thinking. You should know that it is a Kazak, made near the Caucasian–Persian border."

"You've hit it!" Mr. Thacher shouted from under the rug. He emerged and repeated, "You've hit it! It's a typical Kazak!"

"I don't see anything Kazak about it," McMullan protested. "I have a Shirvan with the same pattern in it. I can't go along with these Kazak boys."

"It's either a Kazak or a Kurdistan," said another member.

McMullan was on his knees. "Feel the shortness of the pile. It's undoubtedly a Karabagh."

Mr. Dilley, very calm and gracious, felt the pile and said, "Here's Kazak edging down here."

"Well, you have that in a Karabagh too," McMullan protested.

"There's very obviously," said Mr. Dilley solemnly, "a serious difference of opinion here. Joe thinks it's a Karabagh and I think it's the finest Kazak I ever saw."

McMullan seemed a little shaken. "Well," he said defensively, "I'm just yelling Karabagh because of the scale of these colors."

The proprietor of the store resolved the argument.

"Mr. Dilley is, of course, right. It's one of the finest Kazaks in existence."

After the coffee, brandy, and cigars that follow one of their dinners, the Hajji Babas have a little joke, which, although it has become a custom and lost all elements of surprise, they enjoy still more because of its familiarity. Mr. Dilley rises with gracious dignity and says that he picked up a little piece the other day for which he paid a peddler $40. He hopes that the Hajji Babas will give him their opinion. It is in the next room, waiting their inspection. They know, because it is part of the convention, that Mr. Dilley has borrowed some exquisite museum piece, but they simulate a stunned surprise as they inspect it and congratulate Mr. Dilley for having purchased it for $40.

Hajjis were not happy about what they considered journalistic liberties taken by Mr. Boyer. Dilley himself sought retribution in a paper delivered to the Club later in 1939. The notice of that meeting read, "Another feature of the program will be the reading of a Profile of the Linguistic Magician, Mr. Richard O. Boyer, from the pen of a Ghost (Dilley). Members of the editorial staff of *The New Yorker* have been invited. Attendance of the medical members of the club is particularly requested in consideration of the unusual circumstances."

Early meetings were held at the Harvard Club or in the members' apartments. From the end of the Dilley presidency in 1944 until 1959 meetings were held in various clubs and restaurants. From 1959 to 1971, and since 1978, the regular meeting place has been the National Arts Club on Gramercy Park.

As Boyer suggested in his description of a Hajji gathering, there was a lighthearted spirit in much of what went on. On several occasions, Arthur Dilley wore elaborate silk Persian robes to meetings. Many of these meetings included the presentation of papers, occasionally humorous in nature. In 1939, Harry Weaver gave a paper on Der Kazarian rugs. Der Kazarian was a dealer who specialized in rug repairs, and his shop was stocked with a seemingly limitless supply of rags and tatters used to patch and repair other rugs. As a result, only the most tattered wrecks could be proclaimed true Der Kazarians. Weaver defined the type in this way: "Perhaps the first thing the observer notes about a DerKazarian is its remarkable openwork effect. . . . The claim that it is 'the best ventilated rug in the world' is no idle boast. It anticipates by centuries the modern craze for ventilation and air-conditioning. Hung on a line in the stiffest breeze it will not even tremble. Hung on a wall, it reveals more wall than rug. To some this might be considered a disadvantage, but to the DerKazarian addict it is hailed as a sure and delightful proof of the genuine article."

Most of the papers given at these meetings have been serious studies, however. Tony Lau's paper, "Prolegomena on the Evolution of Some Middle Anatolian Rugs," given at the fourth Club meeting, in December 1932, stands up well to recent studies, with the exception of some slightly optimistic dating. Thacher's March 1939 paper, "XV Century Design in a XIX Century Rug," was re-

Members of the club examining rugs on Hajji Ellis's lawn in 1965.

printed in *The Art Bulletin* later that year. Thacher, who did small repairs on rugs while commuting in the train, as did Olivet, gave a paper on repairs to rugs. Arthur Upham Pope provided a preview of his monumental effort, *The Survey of Persian Art.* More recently, in 1971, Richard Ettinghausen, the eminent art historian and Islamicist, gave a paper on prayer rugs which was expanded to become a catalogue essay for the 1974 Textile Museum exhibition on that subject. Many talks have been given by guest speakers, including such noted scholars as Oleg Grabar of Harvard, Philip Hitti of Princeton, and Dr. Ernst Kühnel. Over the years, probably half to two-thirds of the Club's meetings have included lectures or talks.

The Club has taken great pains to recognize both the seniority and the passing of its members. Memorial programs have been held for McMullan, Dilley, and Thacher, recalling their numerous accomplishments for and on behalf of the Club.

Testimonial programs, citing their loyalty and long years of ardent support, have been held honoring Charles Wilkinson, McMullan, and, most recently, Maurice Dimand, an active member and frequent host and speaker since 1934. Dimand's service to the Club spans so many years that it has now been twenty-three years since his contributions were first recognized, with the Club's gift to the Metropolitan Museum of Art of a seventeenth-century Persian silk brocade in his honor.

The Hajji Baba Club has contributed in many ways to the public's awareness and understanding of Oriental rugs. The Club published, in 1940, Amos Bateman Thacher's *Turkoman Rugs,* a practical guide for collectors and amateurs. All but one or two of the fifty-one rugs illustrated belonged to Club members. Another of Thacher's projects was the compilation of scrapbooks of photographs and discussions of the various rug types which were recognized at that time. These came into the possession of Joe McMullan, who left them to the Textile Museum. They form an incomplete but extremely useful series of documents which may be consulted in the library of that institution.

A 1960 exhibition at the Textile Museum of sixty-two rugs from the collections of Hajji Baba Club members, supplemented by a mimeographed catalogue written by Charles Grant Ellis, gave the public an overview of Hajji interests. In 1966, the Club published *Fine Arts, Including Folly: A History of the Hajji Baba Club, 1932–1960*, by Olive Foster, currently Club secretary. This splendid history contains considerably more detail about the first twenty-eight years of the organization than does the present essay. Also, while the Club itself did not sponsor it, the 1974 exhibition of prayer rugs shown at the Textile Museum and the Montclair Art Museum was brought about through the efforts of several Hajjis, particularly Alvin Pearson and Bruce Westcott.

The public has also benefited from the various accomplishments of individual Hajjis. Maurice Dimand is perhaps best known for his 1973 catalogue, *Oriental Rugs in the Metropolitan Museum of Art*, written with Jean Mailey, currently Club vice-president. He has also organized several rug exhibitions, including *Peasant and Nomad Rugs of Asia*, shown in 1961 at Asia House Gallery, New York.

Charles Grant Ellis, research associate at the Textile Museum, translated the 1958 edition of *Antique Rugs from the Near East*, by Wilhelm von Bode and Ernst Kühnel, indicating in his preface that he sought to make this work "available in some limited form to the inimitable and unfathomable brotherhood of the Hajji Baba Club." Ellis has written extensively for the *Textile Museum Journal* and wrote the catalogue for the exhibition *Early Caucasian Rugs* shown in 1975 at the Textile Museum. His catalogue of the rugs in the Philadelphia Museum of Art is in preparation. Richard Ettinghausen, late chairman of the department of Islamic art at the Metropolitan Museum of Art and professor at the Institute of Fine Arts, New York University, wrote countless articles and books on many aspects of Islamic art history. Louise Mackie of the Royal Ontario Museum in Toronto organized and wrote catalogues for a number of major exhibitions, including *The Splendor of Turkish Weaving* and *Turkmen*, with Jon Thompson, during her years at the Textile Museum.

Several Hajji collections have been catalogued and exhibited. The collection of Michael Kalman, formerly an antiquarian bookseller in Cairo, was shown at the Royal Ontario Museum. The collection of Mary Jane and Jerome Straka, largely donated to the Textile Museum, was catalogued and exhibited there in 1978, and an exhibition of flatweaves from Arthur Jenkins's collection was shown at the Textile Museum in the fall of 1981, with a catalogue prepared by Hajji Cathryn Cootner.

Various Hajjis have given their rugs to institutions for public enjoyment. George Hewitt Myers formed the Textile Museum in Washington, D.C., with his important collection of rugs and textiles. Joseph McMullan divided his rugs among the Textile Museum, the Metropolitan Museum of Art, the Fogg Art Museum, and several other museums. Rugs belonging to the Strakas and to Arthur Jenkins have been given to the Textile Museum, as has Jenkins's extensive library on rugs. H. McCoy Jones has recently donated almost six hundred rugs to the Fine Arts Museums of San Francisco, which plans a series of exhibitions to show different aspects of the collection. Parsons Todd gave his rugs to Macculloch Hall, a historic mansion in Morristown, New Jersey, which he had been restoring and furnishing.

Of all the ways in which Hajjis have shared their knowledge and possessions with the public, one stands out as the most unusual. Charles Grant Ellis once attended a rug auction in New York and watched a woman in the audience successfully bid for a most attractive kilim half. Seeing with dismay that she was not bidding on the other half, which was a different lot, Ellis bought the second half himself for a modest sum, took it over to the woman, and unceremoniously dropped it in her lap, chiding her to see that the halves not be separated in the future. Both halves of this kilim now belong to the Textile Museum, the gift of a grateful auction-goer.

But it is the generous and fraternal dealings of members with each other which have given the Club its special quality over all these years. Dilley's bequest to the Club of the rights to his book is just one example. When Dilley died in 1959, he left part of his personal collection of rugs to his daughter. Eight years later, she decided to sell these rugs and offered them to members of the Club. Several of these rugs have remained within the Club, and one, no. 40 in this exhibition, has been given to an institution.

Arthur Arwine, unable to find a satisfactory way of distributing his fine collection of Turkoman rugs among Hajji members, left them instead to one member, who has honored Arwine's wishes by making them available for other Hajjis to enjoy and by lending generously to exhibitions.

The possibility of Hajjis competing for rugs at auction has been avoided by a ten-section "Plan for Auction Purchase," adopted by the Club in 1939. Such has been the esprit de corps of the Hajji Baba Club.

As the Club begins its second fifty years, it is an appropriate time to reexamine its mission. Dilley, eight years after the founding of the Club, gave a paper at a Club meeting in which he sought to justify its existence and growth. In his characteristically overwrought prose, loaded with pertinent and not so pertinent historical and literary references and quotations, Dilley expounded on the value of the human creative genius, on the West's fascination with the exotica of the East, and on art as the universal language of human understanding. His most telling words, still appropriate today, were about the rugs themselves:

Rugs combine beauty, which is their passport, utility, which constitutes their security, and, to a degree unapproached by any other art, the variables x, y, and z, which are the seeds of the open sesame. Beauty fades and palls, utility wanes, but so long as in rugs flowers repre-

sent the garden of paradise, a tree set in a horn-handled bowl is a cosmological tree, a pointed niche symbolizes a religion, and a dragon represents God and Emperor, so long will mankind enjoy and treasure the works of authors who, with fingers dipped in the vanity cases of flowers, fruits, berries, seeds, butterflies, hummingbirds, and peacocks, wrote their long deep thoughts and the aspirations of their souls. For in the warp and weft of the mentality of rugs, unseen and unsuspected by the untutored, often hidden from us, are the basic religions, philosophies, histories, literatures, and arts of this life. Into this enchanted palace of thought and knowledge all are permitted to enter who learn the password from the rugs of the threshold.

REFERENCES

Boyer, Richard O. "Profiles: No. 1 Picaroon." *The New Yorker*, September 2, 1939, pp. 24–31.

Dilley, Arthur Urbane. *Oriental Rugs and Carpets*. New York: Charles Scribner's Sons, 1931.

Ellis, Charles Grant. *The Hajji Baba Exhibition of Oriental Rugs* (mimeographed exhibition catalogue). Washington, D.C.: The Textile Museum, 1960.

Foster, Olive. *Fine Arts, Including Folly: A History of the Hajji Baba Club, 1932–1960*. New York: Hajji Baba Club, 1966.

Foster, Olive. "The History of the Hajji Baba Club." *Hali* 2 (1979): 54–58.

"Hajji Baba." *The New Yorker*, February 25, 1939, pp. 11–12.

Pickering, William Russell. *"Don't Forget to Smell the Flowers Along the Way": Portraits of Joseph V. McMullan*. New York: The Near Eastern Art Research Center, 1977.

Thacher, Amos Bateman. *Turkoman Rugs*. New York: Hajji Baba Club, 1940.

G L O S S A R Y

Many of the definitions given below have been taken, with minor revisions, from *Prayer Rugs*, an exhibition catalogue by Richard Ettinghausen, Maurice Dimand, Louise W. Mackie, and Charles Grant Ellis published in 1974 by The Textile Museum, Washington, D.C. They are reprinted here with the museum's permission.

abrash   Uneven color changes in the pile, the result of using yarns from different dye lots which, with time, react differently to light.

asmalyk   Pentagonal knotted-pile weavings made in pairs to decorate the flanks of a camel, especially one transporting a bride. *Asmalyk* were displayed in tents on festive occasions and sometimes fitted with a back to function as a bag.

boteh   A cone- or leaf-shaped device popular in textiles and rugs throughout the Middle East; frequently used in an all-over repeating pattern (see nos. 12 and 22).

brocading   A flat-weave technique in which the design of a rug is defined through the use of supplementary wefts. These may be applied in the weft-wrapping technique, sometimes called *sumak*-brocading, in which pattern wefts wrap around warps in a regular, continuous fashion. They may also be applied in the weft-float technique, in which there is no wrapping and supplementary wefts simply float along the back (or are cut) when not needed for the pattern.

chuval   Large, deep bag, used primarily in tents, suspended on the wall from the support structure.

engsi   Knotted-pile tent door rug. Hung on the outside of a tent to cover the doorway.

gul   A small medallion, often octagonal in shape, that is repeated to form the field pattern in many Turkoman carpet weavings. Often two different *guls* are present, one more prominent than the other.

Herati pattern   A small Persian repeat pattern, usually consisting of a central diamond lozenge surrounded by four curved leaves (see no. 21).

kilim   Tapestry-woven rug. Discontinuous colored wefts are woven back and forth in each color area in weft-faced plain weave. Rug specialists refer to kilims as flat-woven rugs to distinguish them from pile rugs.

lazy lines   Diagonal lines, often several inches in length, formed by the meeting points of successive rows of discontinuous wefts of the same color. The discontinuous wefts replace the usually continuous wefts. In pile rugs such lines are clearly visible on the back and also on the upper surface, if it is sufficiently worn.

mafrash   A small bag. Often only the knotted-pile front of the bag survives.

mihrab   Niche in the mosque wall oriented toward Mecca, indicating the direction of prayer; used also to denote the niche design on prayer rugs, although this identification has been questioned.

overcasting   Wrapped material added to the side finish of a rug around the foundation elements.

pile   Yarns that project from the plane of a fabric to form a raised surface. The pile in rugs is composed of the cut ends of the yarns that form the rug knots.

rug knots

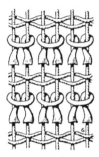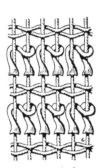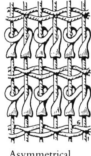

Symmetrical knot. Also called Turkish or Ghiordes knot.

Courtesy C. G. Ellis

Asymmetrical knot open to the left. Also called Persian or Senneh knot.

Courtesy C. G. Ellis

Asymmetrical knot open to the right. Also called Persian or Senneh knot.

R. L. Fisher

shot	The passage of a weft across a fabric. In rugs, one or more weft shots, usually in plain weave, follow each horizontal row of knots.
spandrel	In a prayer rug, that part of the field above the arch.
tauk-nuska	The *gul* design that incorporates H-shaped bird forms, seen particularly in Arabatchi, Ersari, and Yomut weavings.
torba	Shallow bag, used primarily in tents, suspended on the wall from the support structure.
twist, S and Z	The direction of the spin, or twist, of a yarn, which conforms, when viewed in a vertical position, to the diagonal of the letter S or the letter Z.
warp	Yarns running lengthwise in a fabric from one end to the other, which are interlaced at right angles by the wefts, and around which the pile rug knots are wrapped. The warps in rugs are usually tightly spun and plied for strength. The warps are all in one plane, or are moderately or deeply depressed, depending on the weft tension.
weft	Yarns that run crosswise in a fabric from selvedge to selvedge, interlacing the warp at right angles. Unlike rug warps, rug wefts are often somewhat loosely spun and are frequently not plied or very loosely plied. This allows the wefts to be firmly compacted and holds the rug knots securely in place.
Yürük	A term meaning nomad in Turkish, used to describe the numerous tribal entities of Turkey, many of which have not been specifically identified.

SELECTED BIBLIOGRAPHY

ACAR, BELKIS

1978   "Yüncü Nomad Weaving in the Balikesir Re-
        gion of Western Turkey." In *Yörük: The Nomadic
        Weaving Tradition of the Middle East,* ed. A.
        Landreau, pp. 27–31. Pittsburgh: Museum of
        Art, Carnegie Institute.

ACHDJIAN, BERDJ

1981   "Some Flatweaves and Textiles in the Historical
        Museum, Erivan." *Hali,* vol. 4, no. 1, pp.
        20–23.

AMERICAN ART ASSOCIATION

1925   *The V. and L. Benguiat Private Collection of Rare
        Old Rugs.* Dec. 4 and 5 (auction). New York.

ANDREWS, PETER ALFORD

1980   "The Türkmen Tent." In *Turkmen: Tribal
        Carpets and Traditions,* ed. L. Mackie and J.
        Thompson, pp. 41–59. Washington, D.C.: The
        Textile Museum.

ART INSTITUTE OF CHICAGO

1973   *Near Eastern Art in Chicago Collections.* Chicago.

ARTS COUNCIL OF GREAT BRITAIN

1972   *Islamic Carpets from the Joseph V. McMullan
        Collection.* London.

AZADI, SIAWOSCH

1975   *Turkoman Carpets and the Ethnographic Signifi-
        cance of Their Ornaments.* Rev. ed., trans. R.
        Pinner. Fishguard, Wales: Crosby Press.

BIDDER, HANS

1964   *Carpets from Eastern Turkestan.* Trans. Grace
        Marjory Allen. New York: Universe Books.

BLACK, DAVID, AND LOVELESS, CLIVE, EDS.

1979   *Woven Gardens: Nomad and Village Rugs of the
        Fars Province of Southern Persia.* London: David
        Black Oriental Carpets.

BODE, WILHELM VON, AND KÜHNEL, ERNST

1958   *Antique Rugs from the Near East.* 4th rev. ed.,
        trans. C. G. Ellis. Braunschweig: Klinkhardt
        und Biermann.

BOGOLYUBOV, A. A.

1973   *Carpets of Central Asia.* Rev. ed., ed. J. M. A.
        Thompson. Ramsdell, Hampshire: Crosby
        Press.

BRÜGGEMAN, W., AND BÖHMER, H.

1980   *Teppiche der Bauern und Nomaden in Anatolien.*
        Hanover: Verlag Kunst und Antiquitäten.

CAMMANN, SCHUYLER V. R.

1972   "Symbolic Meanings in Oriental Rug Pat-
        terns." *Textile Museum Journal,* vol. 3, no. 3, pp.
        5–54.

DE FRANCHIS, AMEDEO, AND HOUSEGO, JENNY

1975   *Tribal Animal Covers from Iran.* Tehran: Tehran
        Rug Society.

DENNY, WALTER B.

1973   "Anatolian Rugs: An Essay on Method." *Textile
        Museum Journal,* vol. 3, no. 4, pp. 7–25.

1979   *Oriental Rugs.* Washington, D.C.: Smithsonian
        Institution.

DILLEY, ARTHUR URBANE

1959   *Oriental Rugs and Carpets.* Rev. by M. S.
        Dimand. Philadelphia: Lippincott.

DIMAND, MAURICE S.

1940   "A Persian Garden Carpet in the Jaipur Mu-
        seum." *Ars Islamica* 7: 93–96.

1961   *Peasant and Nomad Rugs of Asia*. New York: Asia House Gallery.

DIMAND, MAURICE S., AND MAILEY, JEAN

1973   *Oriental Rugs in the Metropolitan Museum of Art*. New York: The Metropolitan Museum of Art.

EDWARDS, A. CECIL

1953   *The Persian Carpet*. London: Duckworth.

EILAND, MURRAY L.

1976   *Oriental Rugs*. Rev. ed. Boston: New York Graphic Society.

1979   *Chinese and Exotic Rugs*. Boston: New York Graphic Society.

ELLIS, CHARLES GRANT

1960   *The Hajji Baba Exhibition of Oriental Rugs*. Washington, D.C.: The Textile Museum.

1967   *East of Turkestan*. Washington, D.C.: The Textile Museum.

1968   "Chinese Rugs." *Textile Museum Journal*, vol. 2, no. 3, pp. 35–52.

1969   "The Ottoman Prayer Rugs." *Textile Museum Journal,* vol. 2, no. 4, pp. 5–22.

1975   "The 'Lotto' Pattern as a Fashion in Carpets." In *Festschrift für Peter Wilhelm Meister,* ed. Annaliese Ohm and Horst Reber. Hamburg: Hauswedell.

ENDERLEIN, VOLKMAR

1971   "Zwei ägyptische Gebetsteppiche in Islamischen Museum." Staatliche Museen zu Berlin, *Forschungen und Berichte* 13.

ERDMANN, KURT

1962   *Oriental Carpets*. 2d ed., trans. C. G. Ellis. New York: Universe Books.

1970   *Seven Hundred Years of Oriental Carpets*. Ed. Hanna Erdmann, trans. M. H. Beattie and H. Herzog. Berkeley and Los Angeles: University of California Press.

ETTINGHAUSEN, RICHARD; DIMAND, MAURICE; MACKIE, LOUISE W.; AND ELLIS, CHARLES GRANT

1974   *Prayer Rugs*. Washington, D.C.: The Textile Museum.

FRANSES, MICHAEL, AND PINNER, ROBERT

1980   "The Turkoman Khalyk." In *Turkoman Studies I,* ed. R. Pinner and M. Franses, pp. 192–203. London: Oguz Press.

GROTE-HASENBALG, WERNER

1921   *Meisterstücke orientalischer Knüpfkunst*. Berlin.

HARVEY, FRED S.

1981   "Turkoman Rugs in Iran Fifty Years Ago: Recollections." *Hali*, vol. 4, no. 1, pp.7–8.

HEMPEL, ROSE, AND PREYSING, MARITHERES GRÄFIN

1970   *Alte Orient-Teppiche*. Hamburg: Museum für Kunst und Gewerbe.

HOUSEGO, JENNY

1973   "The 19th Century Persian Carpet Boom." *Oriental Art* 19: 169–71.

1978   *Tribal Rugs*. New York: Van Nostrand Reinhold.

JONES, H. MCCOY

1970   *Rugs of the Yomud Tribes*. Washington, D.C.: Washington Hajji Baba.

JONES, H. MCCOY, AND BOUCHER, JEFF W.

1973   *Tribal Rugs from Turkmenistan*. Washington, D.C.: International Hajji Baba Society.

1976   *Rugs of the Yomud Tribes.* Washington, D.C.: International Hajji Baba Society.

JONES, H. McCoy; YOHE, RALPH S.;
AND BOUCHER, JEFF W.

1971   *Persian Tribal Rugs.* Washington, D.C.: Washington Hajji Baba.

KÖNIG, HANS

1975   "Beziehungen zwischen den Teppichen Ostturkestans und Moghulindiens." In *Festschrift für Peter Wilhelm Meister*, ed. Annaliese Ohm and Horst Reber. Hamburg: Hauswedell.

1980   "Ersari Carpets." In *Turkmen: Tribal Carpets and Traditions*, ed. L. Mackie and J. Thompson, pp. 190–202. Washington, D.C.: The Textile Museum.

LANDREAU, ANTHONY N., ED.

1978   *Yörük: The Nomadic Weaving Tradition of the Middle East.* Pittsburgh: Museum of Art, Carnegie Institute.

LANDREAU, ANTHONY N., AND PICKERING, W. R.

1969   *From the Bosporus to Samarkand: Flat-Woven Rugs.* Washington, D.C.: The Textile Museum.

LOGES, WERNER

1980   *Turkoman Tribal Rugs.* Trans. R. Tschebull. London: Allen and Unwin.

LORENTZ, H. A.

1972   *A View of Chinese Rugs from the Seventeenth to the Twentieth Century.* London and Boston: Routledge and Kegan Paul.

MACKIE, LOUISE W., AND THOMPSON, JON, EDS.

1980   *Turkmen: Tribal Carpets and Traditions.* Washington, D.C.: The Textile Museum.

McMULLAN, JOSEPH V.

1965   *Islamic Carpets.* New York: Near Eastern Art Research Center.

MOSHKOVA, V. G.

1980   "Tribal Göl in Turkoman Carpets." In *Turkoman Studies I*, ed. R. Pinner and M. Franses. London: Oguz Press.

PETSOPOULOS, YANNI

1979   *Kilims: Flat-Woven Tapestry Rugs.* New York: Rizzoli.

PINNER, ROBERT,
AND FRANSES, MICHAEL

1980a   "Some Interesting Tekke Products and Their Designs. II. The Bird and Animal Tree Asmalyk." In *Turkoman Studies I*, ed. R. Pinner and M. Franses, pp. 114–33. London: Oguz Press.

PINNER, ROBERT,
AND FRANSES, MICHAEL, EDS.

1980b   *Turkoman Studies I.* London: Oguz Press.

POPE, ARTHUR UPHAM, ED.

1964–77 *A Survey of Persian Art.* Tokyo: Meiji Shobo (reissue of 1938–39 edition).

REED, CHRISTOPHER DUNHAM

1966   *Turkoman Rugs.* Cambridge: Fogg Art Museum.

ROYAL ONTARIO MUSEUM

n.d.   *Oriental Rugs: The Kalman Collection.* Toronto.

SAUNDERS, PETER

1980   *Tribal Visions.* Novau, Calif.: Marin Cultural Center.

SCHÜRMANN, ULRICH

1969   *Central-Asian Rugs.* Frankfurt: Osterreich.

n.d.   *Caucasian Rugs.* London: Allen and Unwin.

SMITHSONIAN INSTITUTION

1966   *Rugs from the Joseph V. McMullan Collection.* Washington, D.C.

SPUHLER, FRIEDRICH; KÖNIG, HANS; AND VOLKMANN, MARTIN

1978   *Old Eastern Carpets: Masterpieces in German Private Collections.* Munich: Verlag Georg D. W. Callwey.

STRAKA, JEROME A., AND MACKIE, LOUISE W., EDS.

1978   *The Oriental Rug Collection of Jerome and Mary Jane Straka.* New York: Jerome A. Straka.

TEXTILE MUSEUM

1963   *Rugs of the Near and Middle East from the Collections of Arthur D. Jenkins and H. McCoy Jones.* Washington, D.C.

1973   *Turkish Rugs from Private Collections.* Washington, D.C.

THACHER, AMOS BATEMAN

1940   *Turkoman Rugs.* New York: Hajji Baba Club.

TSCHEBULL, RAOUL

1971   *Kazak: Carpets of the Caucasus.* New York: Near Eastern Art Research Center.

YETKIN, SERARE

1978   *Early Caucasian Carpets in Turkey.* Trans. A. and A. Mellaarts. London: Oguz Press.

YOHE, RALPH S., AND JONES, H. McCOY, EDS.

1968   *Turkish Rugs.* Washington, D.C.: Washington Hajji Baba.

ZICK, JOHANNA

1961   "Eine Gruppe von Gebetsteppichen und ihre Datierung." *Berliner Museen* 2: 6–14.

CATALOGUE
and
PLATES

1

STAR USHAK RUG

Turkey, late 16th or early 17th century
W. Parsons Todd Foundation,
Macculloch Hall Historical Museum, Morristown, N.J.

Because of their similarity to the more recent production of that area, several related groups of rugs of the sixteenth and seventeenth centuries have been attributed to western Anatolia around the city of Ushak. Contemporary European demand for the early Ushak rugs was keen, and they were frequently depicted in European paintings of the period as obvious symbols of status. European weavers in Flanders or England went so far as to copy Ushak rugs, sometimes incorporating in their designs the coat of arms of the patron commissioning their work. Two such carpets in the Star Ushak design, commissioned by the Montagu family, are dated 1584 and 1585 respectively (Erdman 1970, fig. 262).

Ushak rugs were made in large sizes; this permitted a unit of the field pattern to be repeated one or more times, suggesting an infinite pattern of which we view only a portion through the frame of the border. The pattern generally consisted of rounded medallions or, as in the present case, alternating star- or diamond-shaped medallions arranged in staggered rows. The elevation of such elements to medallion status is a result of Persian influence (the use of a central medallion was de rigueur in many court pieces), but their repetition in a seemingly infinite pattern betrays their Turkish origins.

Because the proportions of this example are not correct, the rug having been shortened and the bottom border replaced, the repetitive nature of the field pattern is not apparent. In other respects, however, this rug is a model of its type. The use of the same ground color in field and border; the emphasis on red and blue; the finely drawn tendrils of the medallions with their twists and knots which contrast with the angular, spindly vines of the field are all features to be expected in such rugs. The border design is not the more characteristic arabesque scrolls and palmettes, however, but a series of palmettes flanked and embraced by forked tendrils. Related designs appear in sixteenth-century Persian silks and carpets (e.g. Branicki hunting rug; Pope 1964–77, pl. 1196), suggesting a possible source for the border design of this rug.

Provenance: ex-collection W. Parsons Todd.

Not previously published.

TECHNICAL DATA
Size: 104¹/₂″ (265.5 cm.) x 80³/₄″ (205 cm.).
Warp: white wool, 2 Z-yarns S-plied, warps even.
Weft: red wool, 1 Z-yarn, 2 shots, lazy lines.
Pile: wool, 2 Z-yarns, symmetrical knot, 8 horiz. x 10 vert. per in. (80 per sq. in./1240 per sq. dm.).
Sides: red wool around 2 warps.
Ends: not original.
Colors (7): red, light blue, dark blue, olive green, beige, dark brown, white.
Condition: rug shortened; main border and inner guard on bottom end replaced to full width of field; parts of outer guard replaced; various repairs throughout.

DOUBLE-NICHE USHAK RUG
Turkey, late 16th century

A group of small rugs has been assigned to Ushak primarily because of perceived similarities in color and in border designs to the larger Ushak types. The border of this rug, for example, consists of a series of floral arabesque arches similar to those decorating the border of a Star Ushak in the Metropolitan Museum of Art (Dimand and Mailey 1973, no. 72). Whether most of these rugs were actually produced in the Ushak region or in Eastern Europe, as has been suggested by Charles Grant Ellis (in correspondence and in Ellis 1975, p. 28), is a question which warrants attention.

Rugs of this class are sometimes referred to as prayer rugs, that is, rugs employed to provide a Muslim with the "clean place" required for prayer five times a day. Such rugs can be identified by the arch or doorway shape in the field, thought by some to suggest the niche or *mihrab* on the wall of the mosque indicating the direction of Mecca and the proper orientation for prayer. Not all niches on rugs are necessarily *mihrabs*, however, and not all prayer rugs necessarily have niche designs. Although this Ushak rug is the right size to be a prayer rug and includes a niche design in the field, unlike a standard prayer rug it also has a second niche design at the opposite end of the field. The second niche, however, lacks the little serrated embellishment, a degenerate form of either a mosque lamp or a vase containing flowers.

Many of the Persian carpets of the sixteenth century had a centralized design with a medallion at the center and quarter medallions at the corners. It is not difficult to imagine that the Ushak weaver, in an effort to "Persianize" his product, utilized forms already familiar to him, particularly the niche design, and combined them in a new way.

An exceptional example of its type, by virtue of its condition, its color, and the clarity of its design, this rug is closely matched by several other pieces, including rugs in the Metropolitan Museum of Art (acc. no. 22.100.111; Dimand and Mailey 1973, no. 83) and in Vienna (Österreichisches Museum für angewandte Kunst, Inv. Nr. T 6943). Kurt Erdmann (1970, p. 155) dates this group to the mid-sixteenth to mid-seventeenth century and places the rugs with cloudbands in the spandrels, as in this piece, in the earlier part of this range.

Provenance: acquired by present owner from an antique dealer in New York in the late 1940s.

Not previously published.

TECHNICAL DATA
Size: 57¹/₂″ (146 cm.) x 46″ (117 cm.).
Warp: red wool, 2 Z-yarns S-plied, alternates moderately depressed.
Weft: red wool, 1 Z-yarn, 2 shots, lazy lines.
Pile: wool, 2 Z-yarns, symmetrical knot, 11 horiz. x 12 vert. per in. (132 per sq. in./2021 per sq. dm.).
Sides: not original.
Ends: warp fringe.
Colors (8): red, medium blue, dark blue, yellow, medium brown, dark brown, beige, white.
Condition: extensive but even wear; several patched or reknotted areas along top and bottom edges and along central axis, particularly in center of medallion; ends worn into pile.

GHIORDES PRAYER RUG
Turkey, 19th century

Ushak carpets represented one level of production, which might be termed a commercial level, with many of the rugs destined for export. Another level was established by the Ottoman court, and finely woven carpets in intricately drawn designs, including prayer rugs, were woven in Istanbul and Bursa in court manufactories. Ottoman rugs (see Ellis 1969) served as models for much of the local production of Anatolia in the eighteenth and nineteenth centuries, and it is sometimes possible to trace the devolution of a design in a series of rugs.

The town of Ghiordes, situated to the west of Ushak, is noted for its eighteenth- and nineteenth-century rugs in prayer-rug designs. Far too many Ghiordes rugs exist, however, and the variety of types associated with that town suggests multiple sources. Bandirma, for example, produced rugs of the Ghiordes type commercially around 1900.

This example is in many respects characteristic of the true Ghiordes type. The key design feature is its squat niche with a stepped, pointed arch, typically framed by a row of small carnations. The design in the spandrel, the area above the niche, traditionally consists of leafy scrolls or rows of small floral units, as are seen on this piece. Two horizontal panels complete the field area, which is surrounded by multiple borders. The palette is broad, but many of the colors are of approximately the same value, resulting in a subtle rather than a dramatic effect. Two technical features may be pointed out as characteristic: the use of white cotton highlights in the pile; and the use of two different weft colors, one through the borders and the other through the field, the two meeting at lazy lines along the sides of the niche.

The absence of design elements carried over from the Ottoman prayer rugs of the late sixteenth and the seventeenth century suggests a nineteenth-century date for this piece. The most unusual feature is the border, a geometrized design seen in one other rug now in Budapest (Iparmüvészeti Múzeum, Inv. Nr. 51.119). Ghiordes borders usually consist of a reciprocal flower-and-curved-leaf pattern taken from Ottoman pieces or, in later rugs, a series of squared-off floral devices repeated in seemingly block-printed fashion.

Provenance: acquired by present owner in the trade in the late 1950s.

Not previously published.

TECHNICAL DATA
Size: 60″ (152 cm.) x 49″ (124.5 cm.).
Warp: off-white wool, 2 Z-yarns S-plied, warps even.
Weft: red wool or white wool (behind field), 1 or 2 Z-yarns, 2 shots, lazy lines.
Pile: wool or white cotton, 1 Z-yarn, symmetrical knot, 9 horiz. x 11 vert. per in. (99 per sq. in./1534 per sq. dm.).
Sides: blue-dyed silk around 3 warps.
Ends: plain weave, warp fringe.
Colors (9): red, orange (virtually indistinguishable from red in places), blue (with *abrash*), light blue (with *abrash*), blue green, light green, yellow, brown (with *abrash*), white.
Condition: woven top end first; a few minor repairs.

4.

KULA PRAYER RUG
Turkey, 19th century

Another western Anatolian town famous for its prayer rugs is Kula, situated between Ushak and the large city of Izmir on the Aegean. Kula prayer rugs display a number of conventions seen in this example. Two vertical bands, degenerate column forms suspended from the spandrel above the niche, are main elements in the niche design. A horizontal panel housing fluttering S-forms tops off the field area and provides visual movement in what is otherwise a static design. Multiple narrow borders, thirteen in this case, frame the field, although in other versions a main border may be utilized along with the narrow ones. Characteristically, the color range emphasizes blue and yellow, but the colors have altered with time. One yellowish shade was originally green, and the dark brown has corroded, exposing the lighter foundation.

As is the case with many Anatolian prayer rugs, this one was woven top end first. The pile of a rug normally leans toward the weaver, and in rugs with directional designs, the weaver often begins at the bottom of the design. Since the pile of this rug leans upward in rela-tion to the design, however, we know the design was formed upside down on the loom. Cammann (1972, p. 20) has suggested that this was done deliberately, so that when the worshipper slid his hands forward, they moved with the pile rather than against it. It is intriguing to note that the central feature of the niche, a composite flowering shrub topped by three pomegranates, grows upside down out of a vase at the top of the niche.

Provenance: ex-collection Mr. and Mrs. Dave Chapman.

Published: Yohe and Jones 1968, no. 40 (belongs with caption to no. 49).

TECHNICAL DATA

Size: 70½″ (179 cm.) x 47¼″ (120 cm.).

Warp: light yellow wool, 2 Z-yarns S-plied, alternates moderately depressed.

Weft: orange to reddish brown wool, 1 or occasionally 2 unplied yarns, 2 or occasionally 3 shots, lazy lines.

Pile: wool, 1 unplied yarn, symmetrical knot, 8 horiz. x 10 vert. per in. (80 per sq. in./1240 per sq. dm.).

Sides: blue-dyed silk around 2 warps.

Ends: warp fringe.

Colors (8): red, light blue, dark blue, green (now yellow green in many areas), yellow, light brown, dark brown, white.

Condition: woven top end first; dark brown corroded; a few small reknotted areas; some restoration to sides; ends worn into pile.

5.
MILAS PRAYER RUG
Turkey, second half of 19th century

In the second half of the nineteenth century, striking prayer rugs with Europeanized designs were made in several Anatolian centers, including Ghiordes, Kirshehir, and Milas. Such rugs merely supplemented the production of rugs in more traditional designs. These Europeanized rugs are called "mejedieh" in the trade, because of the supposed introduction of European styles during the reign of Sultan Abd ul-Mejid (1839–1861). This rug was woven in Milas, a southwestern Anatolian town on the Aegean known for its prayer rugs.

Typical of Milas products in its bright colors and red wefts, this is a most attractive version, although the degeneration of design elements suggests it is not in the earliest group. Other rugs, for example, show the field flanked by columns entwined with winding wreaths. The corresponding vertical border areas in this rug bear no hint of a columnar appearance, but the few scattered diagonal devices remind us of the winding wreaths. The main element of the outer border, clearly depicted in Ladik rugs as a tulip flanked by leaves, is here stylized into a virtually abstract, though pleasing, design.

The identification of the central elements of the field is highly problematic. Other examples have abstract floral designs involving a vertical stem with serrated leaves growing out on diagonals. The weaver of this piece has provided an unusual effect by treating the various parts of such a design as closed compartments, each with a different ground color. An interesting convention is the use of two shades of red, the lighter one employed to outline the main design elements in the field, thus providing sharper contrast than the darker red shade would have. At the top of the niche a jewel-like triangular form is suspended by chains. This derives from the mosque lamps depicted in the niches of much earlier prayer rugs.

Provenance: acquired by present owner at a New York auction in the late 1960s.

Not previously published.

TECHNICAL DATA
Size: 68½" (174 cm.) x 45½" (115.5 cm.).
Warp: white wool, 2 Z-yarns S-plied, alternates slightly depressed.
Weft: red wool, 1 Z-yarn, 3 shots.
Pile: wool, 2 Z-yarns, symmetrical knot, 7½ horiz. x 10 vert. per in. (75 per sq. in./1162 per sq. dm.).
Sides: red wool around 2 cords of 2 warps each; overcasting extends into foundation in form of triangular darts.
Ends: top has plain weave, finished with 5 rows of brocading to which have been attached cloth loops for hanging; bottom has plain weave, warp fringe.
Colors (8): red (2), purple, blue, light green, yellow, dark brown, white.
Condition: a few small rewoven areas.

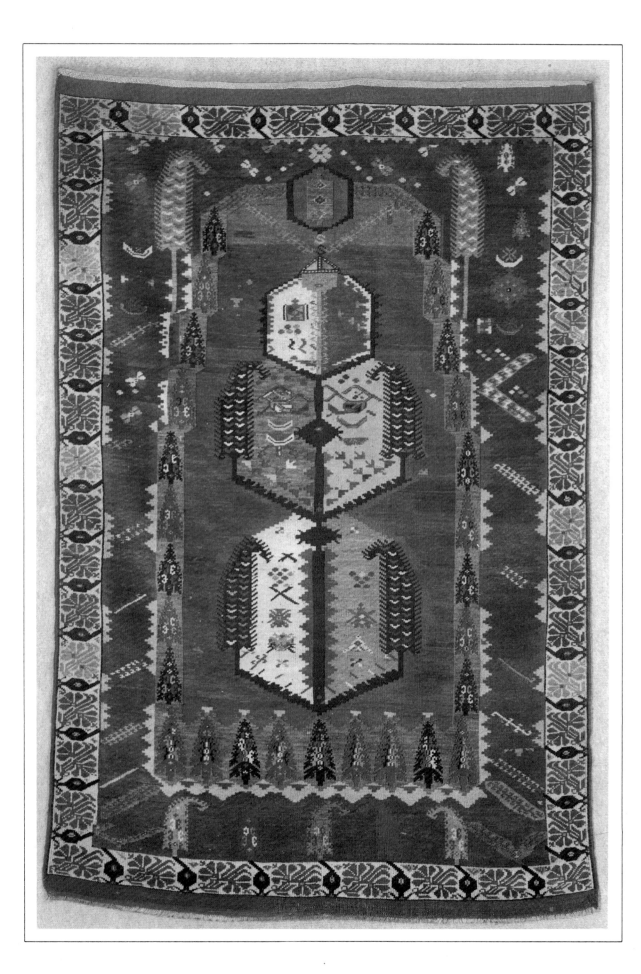

6.

BERGAMA RUG
Turkey, 19th century
The Metropolitan Museum of Art, New York City.
Bequest of Joseph V. McMullan, 1974

This type of rug is known as a "Holbein variant" because earlier rugs of similar design were depicted by the German painter Hans Holbein in the sixteenth century and have long been known in the West by his name. The design of both the original Holbein rugs, of which various examples survive, and the variants is distinguished by the particular design of the medallion, with its concentric geometric shapes and jewel-like or knotted projections. Because the variants such as this have been traditionally attributed to the area around Bergama, a market town built on the site of Hellenistic Pergamon, so too have the original Holbein rugs been assigned to that area. As in the case of Ushak, it is perhaps better to think of Bergama in terms of a class of rug rather than a specific source.

Characterized by a superbly drawn and colored design, the medallion is encircled by a line of octagons containing eight-pointed stars, all on a mint green ground. This green takes on a slightly reddish hue due to the red wefts showing through the pile. In the cor-ners of the field are bracketed devices in coloring similar to that of the medallion. The striking border design consists of a row of reciprocal floral designs made up of a floral calyx and leaves on a brilliant yellow ground. A very similar rug has recently been published (Brüggemann and Böhmer 1980, no. 52). It has the same field design as this rug, but doubled, and it has the same technical features. Such rugs demonstrate that a fine weave is not necessary for a visually exciting result.

Provenance: ex-collection Joseph V. McMullan.

Published: McMullan 1965, no. 97; Yohe and Jones 1968, no. 18; Arts Council of Great Britain 1972, no. 97.

TECHNICAL DATA
Size: 66" (167.5 cm.) x 57" (145 cm.).
Warp: white wool, 2 Z-yarns S-plied, alternates slightly depressed.
Weft: red wool, 1 Z-yarn, 2 shots.
Pile: wool, 2 Z-yarns, symmetrical knot, 6 horiz. x 8 vert. per in. (48 per sq. in./744 per sq. dm.).
Sides: red wool around 4 pairs of warps.
Ends: plain weave, warp fringe.
Colors (6): red, dark blue, light green, yellow, brown, white.
Condition: sides partially restored; brown corroded.

7.
YÜRÜK RUG
Northwestern Turkey, second half of 19th century
The Fine Arts Museums of San Francisco.
H. McCoy Jones Collection

Coarsely woven Anatolian rugs such as this, with thick, fleecy wool and weave and design irregularities, are usually attributed to the nomadic or seminomadic tribes. Because of the vast numbers of these tribes, and because of the lack of information about most of them, the term *Yürük*, meaning "wanderers" in Turkish, has historically been used to describe them. Such Yürük rugs as this, with a somber red and blue palette and a design consisting of diamonds and latchhooks, have recently been associated with the Yüncü nomads of the Balikesir area in northwestern Anatolia. The kilims attributed to this group have been discussed by Belkis Acar. In view of our lack of familiarity with the pile rugs of this people, an attribution simply to northwestern Turkey, tantamount to the familiar Bergama classification, is justified.

Noteworthy qualities of this rug include its almost square proportions; the irregularity in the diamond shapes, particularly in the main border; and the use of sparing quantities of white wool for highlights in both carefully chosen and random spots. The carefully selected area of white is the guard band immediately framing the field. This elaborates a design of end-to-end S-forms seen in earlier Anatolian prayer rugs of undetermined origin, a design which is repeated without white highlights in an outer guard band. The somber palette reminds us of Baluchi weavings from eastern Iran.

A similar rug with a more varied palette has recently been published by Brüggemann and Böhmer (1980, no. 81). Dye analysis indicated that the bluish red is cochineal, suggesting an 1850 to 1890 dating. This is a dating which might be appropriate for this rug as well.

Provenance: ex-collections Michael Kalman, H. McCoy Jones.

Published: Ellis 1960, no. 45; probably Royal Ontario Museum, no. 3 (not illustrated).

TECHNICAL DATA

Size: 77¹/₂″ (197 cm.) x 73″ (185.5 cm.).

Warp: white wool, 2 Z-yarns S-plied, alternates moderately depressed.

Weft: reddish brown wool, 1 Z-yarn, 2–4 shots.

Pile: wool, 2 Z-yarns, symmetrical knot, 7 horiz. x 9¹/₂ vert. per in. (66¹/₂ per sq. in./1030 per sq. dm.).

Sides: blue wool around 5 pairs of warps.

Ends: warp fringe.

Colors (5): red (2), dark blue, dark brown (varies to lighter brown), white.

Condition: sides partially restored; small areas of reknotting; small areas of buckling; uneven wear of brown and red.

8.

KONYA RUG
Turkey, 19th century

Awide variety of village and Yürük weavings come from central Anatolia. Many are attributed to Konya, a large and ancient city that serves as the regional center of commerce and has long been involved in rug weaving. Fragments of thirteenth- and fourteenth-century rugs were found in a mosque there. Since the city is in the center of a large wool-producing area, and since there are numerous nomads in the vicinity, it is not surprising that Konya has produced a broad range of rug types. Common to most of them is the fleecy, lustrous wool seen in this rug.

The design of this piece includes several elements that can also be seen in the rugs of other regions, as well as a distinctive field decoration. The cross-shaped medallion is reminiscent of the centerpieces in the small Ushak rugs (see no. 2), while the corner brackets remind us of the devices employed in one of the Bergama rugs (no. 6). Around the central medallion and actually suspended from it symmetrically about the horizontal axis are triangular, jewel-like devices. It has recently been suggested (Brüggemann and Böhmer 1980, nos. 106, 107) that these fill an amuletic function, to ward off the evil eye, and appear only on prayer rugs. Such devices adorn the fields of prayer rugs and hang singly in the niches (see no. 5), suspended by chains. They are related to earlier designs of mosque lamps but are, at the same time, suggestive of jewelry perhaps intended to serve a similar protective function. There is no reason to believe that such protective devices were confined to prayer rugs.

Provenance: acquired by present owner at a New York City auction in 1964.

Not previously published.

TECHNICAL DATA
Size: 106" (269 cm.) x 58 3/4" (149 cm.).
Warp: white wool, 2 Z-yarns S-plied, warps even.
Weft: white wool, 2 Z-yarns, 2 shots.
Pile: wool, 2 Z-yarns, symmetrical knot, 7 1/2 horiz. x 6 vert. per in. (45 per sq. in./697 per sq. dm.).
Sides: red, yellow wool around 4 single warps, then 2 pairs of warps; overcasting projects into pile in triangular darts; several rows of wefts project into the sides, tapering into triangular darts.
Ends: plain weave, folded and sewn under.
Colors (7): red, blue, green, yellow, medium brown, dark brown, white.
Condition: numerous repairs, especially top left and sides; dark brown corroded.

YÜRÜK RUG
Turkey, Erzerum area, second half of 19th century

This rug represents a type rarely published until a couple of years ago, a type usually described as a Yürük rug perhaps from the Sivas area in eastern Anatolia (Saunders 1980, pl. 50; Eiland 1976, fig. 95b). The type is characterized by thick, luxurious wool; a coarse weave; slightly somber coloring enlivened by the luster of the wool; and a field pattern comprised of diamonds with latchhooks occupying the spaces in a diamond lattice, also edged with latchhooks.

The diamond lattice may be shown in a continuously repeating pattern or, as in this case, divided into horizontal bands. In spite of these divisions and the use of a different color scheme in each band, the pattern itself is still a seemingly infinite one, extending under the small bands crossing the field just as it extends under the main border.

A recently published example of the type (Brüggemann and Böhmer 1980, pl. 89 and p. 113) has been assigned to northeastern Anatolia, specifically the Erzerum area, on the basis of dye analysis. The orange yellow dye was found to be fisetin, one component of which is derived from a plant found only in the Erzerum and Fethiye (southwestern Anatolia) areas. Thus, while it is possible that the dyestuff found its way to Sivas, an attribution to the Erzerum area seems more plausible.

A second published example, virtually identical to this one in terms of technical and design details and coloring (but not border), helps to provide a date (Brüggemann and Böhmer 1980, pl. 90 and pp. 114–15). The light blue-red of the published piece tested to be cochineal, a dye whose use was generally limited to 1850 to 1890. Although it is not known if this rug bears any cochineal, the similarity of technical and design details suggests a contemporary manufacture.

Provenance: acquired by present owner in the New York trade in 1951.

Published: Textile Museum 1973, no. 5.

TECHNICAL DATA

Size: 97" (246.5 cm.) x 56 3/4" (144 cm.).

Warp: white and natural brown wool, 2 Z-yarns (1 each color) S-plied, warps even.

Weft: dark blue wool, 1 yarn with slight Z twist, 4 shots.

Pile: wool, 2 Z-yarns, S-plied, symmetrical knots, 8 horiz. x 9 vert. per in. (72 per sq. in./1116 per sq. dm.).

Sides: wool groups of various colors around cords of 2 and 3 warps.

Ends: warp fringe.

Colors (10): red, orange, orange brown, medium blue, dark blue, blue green, yellow, medium brown, dark brown, white.

Condition: some repair to sides; small areas of reknotting.

2.

DOUBLE-NICHE USHAK RUG
Turkey, late 16th century

A group of small rugs has been assigned to Ushak primarily because of perceived similarities in color and in border designs to the larger Ushak types. The border of this rug, for example, consists of a series of floral arabesque arches similar to those decorating the border of a Star Ushak in the Metropolitan Museum of Art (Dimand and Mailey 1973, no. 72). Whether most of these rugs were actually produced in the Ushak region or in Eastern Europe, as has been suggested by Charles Grant Ellis (in correspondence and in Ellis 1975, p. 28), is a question which warrants attention.

Rugs of this class are sometimes referred to as prayer rugs, that is, rugs employed to provide a Muslim with the "clean place" required for prayer five times a day. Such rugs can be identified by the arch or doorway shape in the field, thought by some to suggest the niche or *mihrab* on the wall of the mosque indicating the direction of Mecca and the proper orientation for prayer. Not all niches on rugs are necessarily *mihrabs*, however, and not all prayer rugs necessarily have niche designs. Although this Ushak rug is the right size to be a prayer rug and includes a niche design in the field, unlike a standard prayer rug it also has a second niche design at the opposite end of the field. The second niche, however, lacks the little serrated embellishment, a degenerate form of either a mosque lamp or a vase containing flowers.

Many of the Persian carpets of the sixteenth century had a centralized design with a medallion at the center and quarter medallions at the corners. It is not difficult to imagine that the Ushak weaver, in an effort to "Persianize" his product, utilized forms already familiar to him, particularly the niche design, and combined them in a new way.

An exceptional example of its type, by virtue of its condition, its color, and the clarity of its design, this rug is closely matched by several other pieces, including rugs in the Metropolitan Museum of Art (acc. no. 22.100.111; Dimand and Mailey 1973, no. 83) and in Vienna (Österreichisches Museum für angewandte Kunst, Inv. Nr. T 6943). Kurt Erdmann (1970, p. 155) dates this group to the mid-sixteenth to mid-seventeenth century and places the rugs with cloud-bands in the spandrels, as in this piece, in the earlier part of this range.

Provenance: acquired by present owner from an antique dealer in New York in the late 1940s.

Not previously published.

TECHNICAL DATA
Size: 57¹/₂" (146 cm.) x 46" (117 cm.).
Warp: red wool, 2 Z-yarns S-plied, alternates moderately depressed.
Weft: red wool, 1 Z-yarn, 2 shots, lazy lines.
Pile: wool, 2 Z-yarns, symmetrical knot, 11 horiz. x 12 vert. per in. (132 per sq. in./2021 per sq. dm.).
Sides: not original.
Ends: warp fringe.
Colors (8): red, medium blue, dark blue, yellow, medium brown, dark brown, beige, white.
Condition: extensive but even wear; several patched or reknotted areas along top and bottom edges and along central axis, particularly in center of medallion; ends worn into pile.

3.

GHIORDES PRAYER RUG
Turkey, 19th century

Ushak carpets represented one level of production, which might be termed a commercial level, with many of the rugs destined for export. Another level was established by the Ottoman court, and finely woven carpets in intricately drawn designs, including prayer rugs, were woven in Istanbul and Bursa in court manufactories. Ottoman rugs (see Ellis 1969) served as models for much of the local production of Anatolia in the eighteenth and nineteenth centuries, and it is sometimes possible to trace the devolution of a design in a series of rugs.

The town of Ghiordes, situated to the west of Ushak, is noted for its eighteenth- and nineteenth-century rugs in prayer-rug designs. Far too many Ghiordes rugs exist, however, and the variety of types associated with that town suggests multiple sources. Bandirma, for example, produced rugs of the Ghiordes type commercially around 1900.

This example is in many respects characteristic of the true Ghiordes type. The key design feature is its squat niche with a stepped, pointed arch, typically framed by a row of small carnations. The design in the spandrel, the area above the niche, traditionally consists of leafy scrolls or rows of small floral units, as are seen on this piece. Two horizontal panels complete the field area, which is surrounded by multiple borders. The palette is broad, but many of the colors are of approximately the same value, resulting in a subtle rather than a dramatic effect. Two technical features may be pointed out as characteristic: the use of white cotton highlights in the pile; and the use of two different weft colors, one through the borders and the other through the field, the two meeting at lazy lines along the sides of the niche.

The absence of design elements carried over from the Ottoman prayer rugs of the late sixteenth and the seventeenth century suggests a nineteenth-century date for this piece. The most unusual feature is the border, a geometrized design seen in one other rug now in Budapest (Iparmüvészeti Múzeum, Inv. Nr. 51.119). Ghiordes borders usually consist of a reciprocal flower-and-curved-leaf pattern taken from Ottoman pieces or, in later rugs, a series of squared-off floral devices repeated in seemingly block-printed fashion.

Provenance: acquired by present owner in the trade in the late 1950s.

Not previously published.

TECHNICAL DATA

Size: 60″ (152 cm.) x 49″ (124.5 cm.).
Warp: off-white wool, 2 Z-yarns S-plied, warps even.
Weft: red wool or white wool (behind field), 1 or 2 Z-yarns, 2 shots, lazy lines.
Pile: wool or white cotton, 1 Z-yarn, symmetrical knot, 9 horiz. x 11 vert. per in. (99 per sq. in./1534 per sq. dm.).
Sides: blue-dyed silk around 3 warps.
Ends: plain weave, warp fringe.
Colors (9): red, orange (virtually indistinguishable from red in places), blue (with *abrash*), light blue (with *abrash*), blue green, light green, yellow, brown (with *abrash*), white.
Condition: woven top end first; a few minor repairs.

4.
KULA PRAYER RUG
Turkey, 19th century

Another western Anatolian town famous for its prayer rugs is Kula, situated between Ushak and the large city of Izmir on the Aegean. Kula prayer rugs display a number of conventions seen in this example. Two vertical bands, degenerate column forms suspended from the spandrel above the niche, are main elements in the niche design. A horizontal panel housing fluttering S-forms tops off the field area and provides visual movement in what is otherwise a static design. Multiple narrow borders, thirteen in this case, frame the field, although in other versions a main border may be utilized along with the narrow ones. Characteristically, the color range emphasizes blue and yellow, but the colors have altered with time. One yellowish shade was originally green, and the dark brown has corroded, exposing the lighter foundation.

As is the case with many Anatolian prayer rugs, this one was woven top end first. The pile of a rug normally leans toward the weaver, and in rugs with directional designs, the weaver often begins at the bottom of the design. Since the pile of this rug leans upward in rela-tion to the design, however, we know the design was formed upside down on the loom. Cammann (1972, p. 20) has suggested that this was done deliberately, so that when the worshipper slid his hands forward, they moved with the pile rather than against it. It is intriguing to note that the central feature of the niche, a composite flowering shrub topped by three pomegranates, grows upside down out of a vase at the top of the niche.

Provenance: ex-collection Mr. and Mrs. Dave Chapman.

Published: Yohe and Jones 1968, no. 40 (belongs with caption to no. 49).

TECHNICAL DATA
Size: 70 1/2" (179 cm.) x 47 1/4" (120 cm.).
Warp: light yellow wool, 2 Z-yarns S-plied, alternates moderately depressed.
Weft: orange to reddish brown wool, 1 or occasionally 2 unplied yarns, 2 or occasionally 3 shots, lazy lines.
Pile: wool, 1 unplied yarn, symmetrical knot, 8 horiz. x 10 vert. per in. (80 per sq. in./1240 per sq. dm.).
Sides: blue-dyed silk around 2 warps.
Ends: warp fringe.
Colors (8): red, light blue, dark blue, green (now yellow green in many areas), yellow, light brown, dark brown, white.
Condition: woven top end first; dark brown corroded; a few small reknotted areas; some restoration to sides; ends worn into pile.

MILAS PRAYER RUG
Turkey, second half of 19th century

In the second half of the nineteenth century, striking prayer rugs with Europeanized designs were made in several Anatolian centers, including Ghiordes, Kirshehir, and Milas. Such rugs merely supplemented the production of rugs in more traditional designs. These Europeanized rugs are called "mejedieh" in the trade, because of the supposed introduction of European styles during the reign of Sultan Abd ul-Mejid (1839–1861). This rug was woven in Milas, a southwestern Anatolian town on the Aegean known for its prayer rugs.

Typical of Milas products in its bright colors and red wefts, this is a most attractive version, although the degeneration of design elements suggests it is not in the earliest group. Other rugs, for example, show the field flanked by columns entwined with winding wreaths. The corresponding vertical border areas in this rug bear no hint of a columnar appearance, but the few scattered diagonal devices remind us of the winding wreaths. The main element of the outer border, clearly depicted in Ladik rugs as a tulip flanked by leaves, is here stylized into a virtually abstract, though pleasing, design.

The identification of the central elements of the field is highly problematic. Other examples have abstract floral designs involving a vertical stem with serrated leaves growing out on diagonals. The weaver of this piece has provided an unusual effect by treating the various parts of such a design as closed compartments, each with a different ground color. An interesting convention is the use of two shades of red, the lighter one employed to outline the main design elements in the field, thus providing sharper contrast than the darker red shade would have. At the top of the niche a jewel-like triangular form is suspended by chains. This derives from the mosque lamps depicted in the niches of much earlier prayer rugs.

Provenance: acquired by present owner at a New York auction in the late 1960s.

Not previously published.

TECHNICAL DATA
Size: 68½" (174 cm.) x 45½" (115.5 cm.).
Warp: white wool, 2 Z-yarns S-plied, alternates slightly depressed.
Weft: red wool, 1 Z-yarn, 3 shots.
Pile: wool, 2 Z-yarns, symmetrical knot, 7½ horiz. x 10 vert. per in. (75 per sq. in./1162 per sq. dm.).
Sides: red wool around 2 cords of 2 warps each; overcasting extends into foundation in form of triangular darts.
Ends: top has plain weave, finished with 5 rows of brocading to which have been attached cloth loops for hanging; bottom has plain weave, warp fringe.
Colors (8): red (2), purple, blue, light green, yellow, dark brown, white.
Condition: a few small rewoven areas.

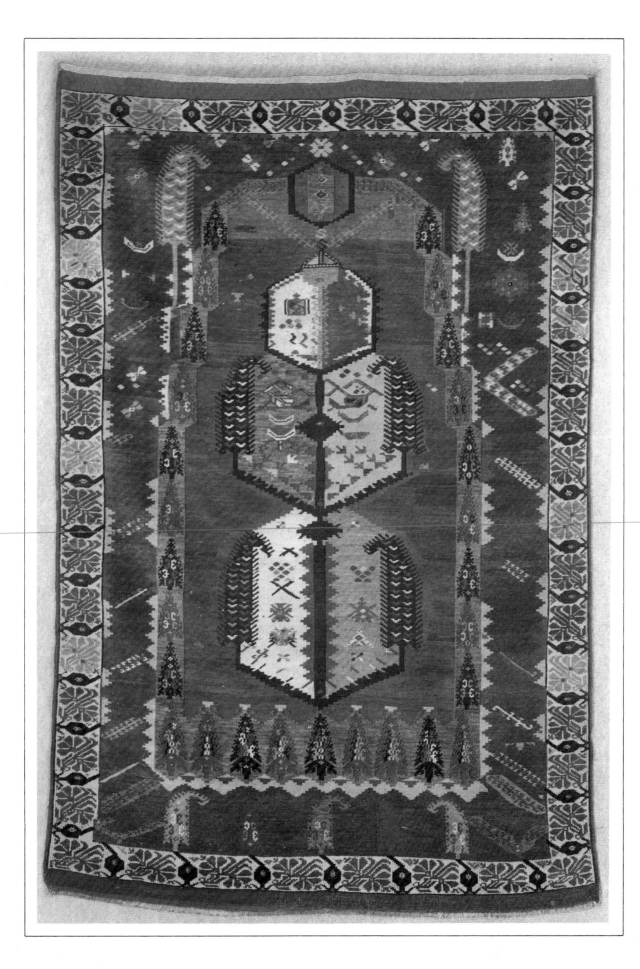

6.

BERGAMA RUG

Turkey, 19th century
The Metropolitan Museum of Art, New York City.
Bequest of Joseph V. McMullan, 1974

This type of rug is known as a "Holbein variant" because earlier rugs of similar design were depicted by the German painter Hans Holbein in the sixteenth century and have long been known in the West by his name. The design of both the original Holbein rugs, of which various examples survive, and the variants is distinguished by the particular design of the medallion, with its concentric geometric shapes and jewel-like or knotted projections. Because the variants such as this have been traditionally attributed to the area around Bergama, a market town built on the site of Hellenistic Pergamon, so too have the original Holbein rugs been assigned to that area. As in the case of Ushak, it is perhaps better to think of Bergama in terms of a class of rug rather than a specific source.

Characterized by a superbly drawn and colored design, the medallion is encircled by a line of octagons containing eight-pointed stars, all on a mint green ground. This green takes on a slightly reddish hue due to the red wefts showing through the pile. In the cor-ners of the field are bracketed devices in coloring similar to that of the medallion. The striking border design consists of a row of reciprocal floral designs made up of a floral calyx and leaves on a brilliant yellow ground. A very similar rug has recently been published (Brügge-mann and Böhmer 1980, no. 52). It has the same field design as this rug, but doubled, and it has the same technical features. Such rugs demonstrate that a fine weave is not necessary for a visually exciting result.

Provenance: ex-collection Joseph V. McMullan.

Published: McMullan 1965, no. 97; Yohe and Jones 1968, no. 18; Arts Council of Great Britain 1972, no. 97.

TECHNICAL DATA
Size: 66″ (167.5 cm.) x 57″ (145 cm.).
Warp: white wool, 2 Z-yarns S-plied, alternates slightly depressed.
Weft: red wool, 1 Z-yarn, 2 shots.
Pile: wool, 2 Z-yarns, symmetrical knot, 6 horiz. x 8 vert. per in. (48 per sq. in./744 per sq. dm.).
Sides: red wool around 4 pairs of warps.
Ends: plain weave, warp fringe.
Colors (6): red, dark blue, light green, yellow, brown, white.
Condition: sides partially restored; brown corroded.

7.

YÜRÜK RUG

Northwestern Turkey, second half of 19th century
The Fine Arts Museums of San Francisco.
H. McCoy Jones Collection

Coarsely woven Anatolian rugs such as this, with thick, fleecy wool and weave and design irregularities, are usually attributed to the nomadic or seminomadic tribes. Because of the vast numbers of these tribes, and because of the lack of information about most of them, the term *Yürük*, meaning "wanderers" in Turkish, has historically been used to describe them. Such Yürük rugs as this, with a somber red and blue palette and a design consisting of diamonds and latchhooks, have recently been associated with the Yüncü nomads of the Balikesir area in northwestern Anatolia. The kilims attributed to this group have been discussed by Belkis Acar. In view of our lack of familiarity with the pile rugs of this people, an attribution simply to northwestern Turkey, tantamount to the familiar Bergama classification, is justified.

Noteworthy qualities of this rug include its almost square proportions; the irregularity in the diamond shapes, particularly in the main border; and the use of sparing quantities of white wool for highlights in both carefully chosen and random spots. The carefully selected area of white is the guard band immediately framing the field. This elaborates a design of end-to-end S-forms seen in earlier Anatolian prayer rugs of undetermined origin, a design which is repeated without white highlights in an outer guard band. The somber palette reminds us of Baluchi weavings from eastern Iran.

A similar rug with a more varied palette has recently been published by Brüggemann and Böhmer (1980, no. 81). Dye analysis indicated that the bluish red is cochineal, suggesting an 1850 to 1890 dating. This is a dating which might be appropriate for this rug as well.

Provenance: ex-collections Michael Kalman, H. McCoy Jones.

Published: Ellis 1960, no. 45; probably Royal Ontario Museum, no. 3 (not illustrated).

TECHNICAL DATA

Size: 77½" (197 cm.) x 73" (185.5 cm.).

Warp: white wool, 2 Z-yarns S-plied, alternates moderately depressed.

Weft: reddish brown wool, 1 Z-yarn, 2–4 shots.

Pile: wool, 2 Z-yarns, symmetrical knot, 7 horiz. x 9½ vert. per in. (66½ per sq. in./1030 per sq. dm.).

Sides: blue wool around 5 pairs of warps.

Ends: warp fringe.

Colors (5): red (2), dark blue, dark brown (varies to lighter brown), white.

Condition: sides partially restored; small areas of reknotting; small areas of buckling; uneven wear of brown and red.

KONYA RUG
Turkey, 19th century

A wide variety of village and Yürük weavings come from central Anatolia. Many are attributed to Konya, a large and ancient city that serves as the regional center of commerce and has long been involved in rug weaving. Fragments of thirteenth- and fourteenth-century rugs were found in a mosque there. Since the city is in the center of a large wool-producing area, and since there are numerous nomads in the vicinity, it is not surprising that Konya has produced a broad range of rug types. Common to most of them is the fleecy, lustrous wool seen in this rug.

The design of this piece includes several elements that can also be seen in the rugs of other regions, as well as a distinctive field decoration. The cross-shaped medallion is reminiscent of the centerpieces in the small Ushak rugs (see no. 2), while the corner brackets remind us of the devices employed in one of the Bergama rugs (no. 6). Around the central medallion and actually suspended from it symmetrically about the horizontal axis are triangular, jewel-like devices. It has recently been suggested (Brüggemann and Böhmer 1980, nos. 106, 107) that these fill an amuletic function, to ward off the evil eye, and appear only on prayer rugs. Such devices adorn the fields of prayer rugs and hang singly in the niches (see no. 5), suspended by chains. They are related to earlier designs of mosque lamps but are, at the same time, suggestive of jewelry perhaps intended to serve a similar protective function. There is no reason to believe that such protective devices were confined to prayer rugs.

Provenance: acquired by present owner at a New York City auction in 1964.

Not previously published.

TECHNICAL DATA
Size: 106″ (269 cm.) x 58³⁄₄″ (149 cm.).
Warp: white wool, 2 Z-yarns S-plied, warps even.
Weft: white wool, 2 Z-yarns, 2 shots.
Pile: wool, 2 Z-yarns, symmetrical knot, 7¹⁄₂ horiz. x 6 vert. per in. (45 per sq. in./697 per sq. dm.).
Sides: red, yellow wool around 4 single warps, then 2 pairs of warps; overcasting projects into pile in triangular darts; several rows of wefts project into the sides, tapering into triangular darts.
Ends: plain weave, folded and sewn under.
Colors (7): red, blue, green, yellow, medium brown, dark brown, white.
Condition: numerous repairs, especially top left and sides; dark brown corroded.

YÜRÜK RUG
Turkey, Erzerum area, second half of 19th century

This rug represents a type rarely published until a couple of years ago, a type usually described as a Yürük rug perhaps from the Sivas area in eastern Anatolia (Saunders 1980, pl. 50; Eiland 1976, fig. 95b). The type is characterized by thick, luxurious wool; a coarse weave; slightly somber coloring enlivened by the luster of the wool; and a field pattern comprised of diamonds with latchhooks occupying the spaces in a diamond lattice, also edged with latchhooks.

The diamond lattice may be shown in a continuously repeating pattern or, as in this case, divided into horizontal bands. In spite of these divisions and the use of a different color scheme in each band, the pattern itself is still a seemingly infinite one, extending under the small bands crossing the field just as it extends under the main border.

A recently published example of the type (Brüggemann and Böhmer 1980, pl. 89 and p. 113) has been assigned to northeastern Anatolia, specifically the Erzerum area, on the basis of dye analysis. The orange yellow dye was found to be fisetin, one component of which is derived from a plant found only in the Erzerum and Fethiye (southwestern Anatolia) areas. Thus, while it is possible that the dyestuff found its way to Sivas, an attribution to the Erzerum area seems more plausible.

A second published example, virtually identical to this one in terms of technical and design details and coloring (but not border), helps to provide a date (Brüggemann and Böhmer 1980, pl. 90 and pp. 114–15). The light blue-red of the published piece tested to be cochineal, a dye whose use was generally limited to 1850 to 1890. Although it is not known if this rug bears any cochineal, the similarity of technical and design details suggests a contemporary manufacture.

Provenance: acquired by present owner in the New York trade in 1951.

Published: Textile Museum 1973, no. 5.

TECHNICAL DATA
Size: 97″ (246.5 cm.) x 56¾″ (144 cm.).
Warp: white and natural brown wool, 2 Z-yarns (1 each color) S-plied, warps even.
Weft: dark blue wool, 1 yarn with slight Z twist, 4 shots.
Pile: wool, 2 Z-yarns, S-plied, symmetrical knots, 8 horiz. x 9 vert. per in. (72 per sq. in./1116 per sq. dm.).
Sides: wool groups of various colors around cords of 2 and 3 warps.
Ends: warp fringe.
Colors (10): red, orange, orange brown, medium blue, dark blue, blue green, yellow, medium brown, dark brown, white.
Condition: some repair to sides; small areas of reknotting.

18.

BROCADED COVER

Southeastern Caucasus or northwestern Iran, dated A.H.1329/A.D. 1911

This cover for floor or bedding was made in a combination of techniques, with weft-wrap brocaded decoration applied to a slit-tapestry ground. The latter technique was necessary to permit the use of more than one ground color, in this case red and blue, which, along with narrow borders, organizes the pattern into distinct areas.

The brocaded decoration consists of two different compositions alternating or repeating in tile fashion throughout the red and blue bands. One shows three creatures of different sizes in a fixed arrangement but facing in alternating directions. Extravagant tail plumage, consisting of diagonal then horizontal lines, and candelabra-like crests projecting from the heads suggest exotic bird species. The second composition is more stylized and difficult to decipher. A large geometric device stands in the center of its rectangle, supported on a vertical stem. Diagonal lines sprout upward from a central diamond. A floral motif is most likely represented here. Flanking this elaborate creation are two small figures suggestive of squatting humans. A date in Arabic numerals corresponding to 1911 is seen just above the center of the cover.

Brocaded covers of this type have been credited (Housego 1978, pls. 5, 13, 14) to a group of Turkish tribes known as the Shahsavan, meaning "those who love the Shah," some of whom reside on the Moghan steppe which straddles the Soviet–Iranian border.

Provenance: ex-collection Mr. and Mrs. Dave Chapman.

Published: Landreau and Pickering 1969, no. 95.

TECHNICAL DATA
Size: 74 ¾″ (190 cm.) × 51½″ (131 cm.).
Technique: weft-wrap brocading on tapestry-weave ground.
Warp: red orange and blue wool (grouped), 3 Z-yarns S-plied, 24 per in.
Weft: red orange and blue wool, 2 Z-yarns S-plied.
Pattern weft: wool, 2 Z-yarns S-plied; white cotton, 3 Z-yarns S-plied.
Sides: red orange wool around 2 warps.
Ends: knotted warp fringe.
Colors (7): red orange, dark blue, light blue-green, dark green, yellow, brown, white.
Condition: excellent.

19.

BROCADED PANEL
Southern Caucasus or northwestern Iran, late 19th or early
20th century

Small bags and bag panels with all-over weft-wrap brocading, particularly ones bearing strange beasts or birds, have traditionally been assigned to the Caucasus (see Landreau and Pickering 1969, no. 66) or, more recently, to the Kurds or Shahsavan of northwestern Iran (Housego 1978, pls. 39, 40). A recent article included a cradle (Achdjian 1981, no. 4) made in the same technique. The design of the cradle panel is extremely similar to the panel shown here, although the creatures are stylized in a somewhat different way. The central horizontal band is filled with the same halved and whole diamond forms edged with latchhooks. This, and several other cradles in the historical museum of Yerevan, have been attributed to Artzukh Province in the Karabakh region of the southern Caucasus. A term sometimes used to describe this technique, *sumak*-brocading,

was first applied specifically to Caucasian pieces. Since many non-Caucasian examples in this technique are now recognized, the use of the term can be misleading.

Provenance: ex-collection Anton Lau.

Published: Landreau and Pickering 1969, no. 66.

TECHNICAL DATA
Size: 20″ (50.5 cm.) × 32³/₄″ (83 cm.).
Technique: all-over weft-wrap brocading.
Warp: white wool, 3 Z-yarns S-plied, 20 per in.
Weft: white wool, 2 Z-yarns S-plied.
Pattern weft: wool, 2 Z-yarns S-plied.
Sides: pattern weft around 2 warps.
Ends: warp fringe.
Colors (9): red, orange red, light orange, dark blue, medium blue, light green, yellow, brown, white.
Condition: pattern weft worn through in a few small areas, exposing foundation; wear at bottom end extends into pattern.

20.

GARDEN RUG

Northwestern Iran, late 18th or early 19th century
Fogg Art Museum, Harvard University, Cambridge, Mass.
Gift of Joseph V. McMullan

Representations of gardens have played an important role in the imagery of Islamic Iran, in both literary and visual media. On the visual side, there is no more commonly found decorative convention than the scrolling vine with blossoms and leaves, either as background for a medallion or as the principal focus of the decoration. Paradise, the word itself of Persian origin, was equated with a garden by the poets and, most importantly, in the Koran, where Paradise was said to contain four gardens, each with a fountain or spring (*surah* 55, verses 46 and 62).

Most visual representations of gardens, or Paradise, are metaphoric in nature and consist of various foliate forms used in a decorative manner. There is, however, a series of Persian rugs which recreate the garden in a more literal form. The formal Persian garden was laid out in a four-part plan, based on the passage in the Koran. The tombs of the Moghul rulers were also designed in a similar fashion, with canals of water separating the four parts, in an attempt to provide the souls of the deceased with gardens of Paradise (discussed by Cammann 1972, pp. 49–50). Such a garden is depicted in an aerial view in an early seventeenth-century rug made in the Kerman area, in southeastern Iran (Dimand 1940).

In the eighteenth and perhaps the early nineteenth centuries a series of rugs evidently based on this prototype was woven in northwestern Iran. Earlier ones show the full four-part garden with main canals crossing at a central square pool (Erdmann 1970, fig. 70) and subsidiary canals coursing through each garden quadrant under circular central plots from which plane trees grow. The later group of rugs, to which the present example belongs, shows one-quarter of the original four-part plan. This garden is subdivided by canals with rippling water and fish whose scales are indicated with colored dots of yarn. Each subdivision contains two rectangular areas, one of which serves as a background for the plane trees that grow out of the central raised terraces over the canal. There is a curious mixture of spatial viewpoints here, with the garden sections seen from an aerial standpoint and the plane trees and individual flowers, particularly those in the beds framing each subdivision, shown in profile.

The field of this rug is quite worn, but sufficient pile remains at the borders to support the Kurdish, or northwest Persian, attribution. The wool of this region is particularly lustrous and soft. There are a number of rugs closely related to this one, including an example in the Museum für Islamische Kunst, West Berlin (Inv. Nr. I. 41/69) and one in the Metropolitan Museum of Art (acc. no. 67.156; Dimand and Mailey 1973, no. 45).

Provenance: ex-collection Joseph V. McMullan.

Published: McMullan 1965, no. 29; Smithsonian Institution 1966, no. 16; Arts Council of Great Britain 1972, no. 29.

TECHNICAL DATA

Size: 267¹/₂″ (680 cm.) × 95¹/₂″ (242.5 cm.). Detail shown.
Warp: white cotton, 5 Z-yarns S-plied, warps even.
Weft: light red wool, 2 Z-yarns S-plied, 2 shots.
Pile: wool, 2 Z-yarns, symmetrical knots, 8 horiz. × 9 vert. per in. (72 per sq. in./1116 per sq. dm.).
Sides: red wool around cords of 2 and 3 warps.
Ends: warp fringe.
Colors (14): red (3), red brown, pink, purple, medium blue, dark blue, blue green, light green, dark green, yellow, dark brown, white.
Condition: worn and repaired area in field at top end of rug; various areas of repair and reknotting through field, apparent because of color changes; field more worn than border.

21.
SENNEH RUG
Iran, mid-19th century
The Textile Museum, Washington, D.C.
Bequest of Fred L. Kramer

The city of Sanandaj, formerly Senneh, is the capital of Iranian Kurdistan. It is a busy trading center and, at least since the nineteenth century, has been famous for its rug weaving. Senneh was described in 1854 as producing the finest Persian carpets, and rugs from Senneh were shown at the 1873 International Exposition at Vienna (cited Housego 1973, p. 170).

The pile rugs of Senneh are notable for their exceedingly fine weave, on a foundation of cotton and sometimes silk; for the use of a pistachio green color seen also in the rugs of Feraghan; and for their reliance on all-over repeat patterns, sometimes seen employed in a medallion format. All of these qualities are found in this example. The small-scale pattern, the so-called Herati pattern of a central diamond form flanked by four curved leaves, is repeated in offset rows, continuing in regular fashion even through the color changes from medallion to field to corner areas. The boundaries of these parts of the design serve only to separate the colors of the ground. The extremely thin pile, fine weave, and small-scale repeating pattern suggest a strong textile influence.

Provenance: ex-collection Fred L. Kramer.

Not previously published.

TECHNICAL DATA
Size: 92" (233.5 cm.) × 51³/₄" (131.5 cm.).
Warp: White silk, 3 Z-yarns S-plied, alternates moderately
    depressed.
Weft: white cotton, 4 Z-yarns S-plied, 1 shot.
Pile: wool, 2 Z-yarns, symmetrical knot, 19 horiz. × 16 vert.
    (approx.) per in. (304 per sq. in./4712 per sq. dm.).
Sides: purple wool around 2 warps and a multistrand cotton cable.
Ends: several rows of brocading, then warp fringe.
Colors (8): red, pink, dark blue, light blue, light green, yellow,
    black, white.
Condition: a few minor repairs in field and at ends; sides curl;
    colors brighter on back.

22

SENNEH KILIM
Iran, second half of 19th century

Senneh is at least as well known for its slit-tapestry weavings as for its pile rugs. This example is a particularly finely woven kilim on a foundation of cotton and wool. Well-drawn *botehs*, briefly discussed in catalogue entry no. 12, are aligned in offset rows in a repeating pattern which can be seen continuing under the border. Each *boteh* consists of a central vertical stem in green with an array of symmetrically disposed leaves and roses. The entire composition is outlined in tiny white buds which stand out in sharp contrast to the dark blue ground. The direction of each row of *botehs* alternates. A narrow border of leaves and a scrolling vine frame the field.

The *boteh* was but one of several small-scale motifs used to make up the repeating patterns seen on Senneh kilims. The Herati pattern, seen on no. 21, was popular, and so were both diagonal and vertical narrow stripes containing scrolling vines. These elements, in fact, tend to be used interchangeably in the different parts of the kilim designs. *Botehs* may be seen in the main border, when there is one, or in the spandrels above a niche. Stripes may fill the field or, in the case of diagonal ones, the main border. The Herati pattern, however, tends to be restricted to the field. There are other small motifs used as well.

Provenance: acquired by present owner in the New York trade in 1971.

Published: Jones, Yohe, and Boucher 1971, no. 3.

TECHNICAL DATA
Size: 59″ (150 cm.) × 49½″ (125.5 cm.).
Technique: slit tapestry.
Warp: white cotton, 4 Z-yarns S-plied, 30 per in.
Weft: wool, 2 Z-yarns S-plied.
Sides: no overcasting.
Ends: plain weave with brocaded stripe, then braided warp fringe.
Colors (8): red, pink, dark blue, light blue, green, yellow, brown, white.
Condition: slight wear at sides.

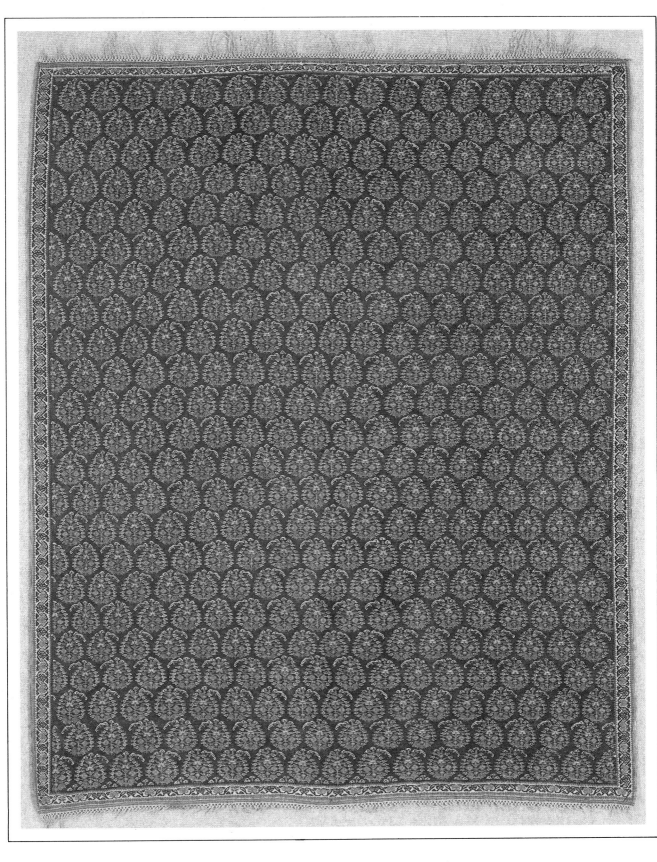

23

BROCADED HORSE COVER
Northwestern Iran, late 19th or early 20th century
The Textile Museum, Washington, D.C.
Gift of Jerome and Mary Jane Straka

Horse covers are a necessary functional item among the various tribal groups of Iran. Usually of this shape, with two long horizontal extensions which were joined under the horse's neck, the piece would lie across the horse's back over the saddle, the braided fringe swaying at the rear, accentuating the motion of the animal.

This cover is woven in a weft-float brocading technique, in which the pattern wefts not seen on the front side are carried across the back. The arms which join under the horse's neck are visually extended the full length of the piece in stripes of varying ground color. In spite of the illusion created by these stripes, the cover was woven in one piece. Between the two sets of stripes is a stepped polygon filled with rows of small geometric devices. The dark blue medallion sits on a field of the same ground color, filled with rows of another geometric device which resembles the *boteh*. Additional geometric elements are brocaded on the stripes flanking the field. Top and bottom ends are finished with unusual multicolored stripes with an overall diamond pattern, achieved by floating the wefts on the front instead of the back.

Horse covers were made in several joined pieces by the Shahsavan. The Luri and the Qashqai of Fars Province, near Shiraz in southern Iran, wove horse covers decorated in both weft-wrap and weft-float brocading techniques. This example seems closest to one published by de Franchis and Housego (1975, no. 8), of a type said to appear in the bazaars of Qazvin and Bijar. The authors attribute that piece to the Khamseh district of northwestern Iran.

Provenance: ex-collection Jerome A. and Mary Jane Straka.

Published: Straka and Mackie 1978, no. 91.

TECHNICAL DATA
Size: 67″ (170 cm.) × 55″ (140 cm.), excluding fringe.
Technique: weft-float brocading on plain-weave ground.
Warp: blue, red, light orange, white wool, 2 Z-yarns S-plied.
Weft: wool, 2 Z-yarns S-plied.
Pattern weft: wool, 2 Z-yarns.
Sides: gold and brown, red and blue green wool, checkerboard fashion, around 8 warps.
Ends: top has warp fringe in loops; bottom has braided and knotted warp fringe groups.
Colors (10): red, light orange, medium blue, dark blue, blue green, gold, beige, brown, black, white.
Condition: excellent.

24.

KILIM

Iran, Saveh–Qazvin area, late 19th or early 20th century

Iranian kilims have much in common with their Caucasian counterparts. Distinguishing the two can, in fact, be difficult in some cases. Generally speaking, Iranian tapestry-woven pieces, excluding the Senneh products, tend to be more coarsely woven and to employ many diamond forms, usually serrated ones, in their design. In this striking piece serrated diamonds are employed in characteristic fashion in offset or diagonal rows with random coloring. Each diamond contains concentric diamonds with triangular projections, some of the diamonds outlined in a contrasting color. Sometimes these geometric elements are of primary importance, as here, and sometimes they are secondary to larger, different forms.

Although we inevitably analyze the major elements of the field in trying to trace the origins of a piece, this can be misleading because it is precisely these major motifs and design elements which may have been borrowed from other sources. Secondary elements, which are less likely to be incorporated from outside sources, are sometimes a more reliable indicator of origin. So it is in this case. Kilims published by Housego (1978, pl. 36) and Petsopoulos (1979, pl. 365) have a common origin with the rug shown here, as is evident from their guard bands, with a continuous design of small diamonds and bars in one and continuous connected diamonds in the other, and from their end finishes, with brocaded stripes added to the plain-weave skirts. This kilim belongs to a type said by Housego to be from villages between Saveh and Qazvin, just west of Tehran. Settled Shahsavan tribes make up part of the population of these villages. Such pieces are often called Zarand kilims in the trade, after a particular village in this area.

Provenance: acquired by present owner in the New York trade in 1972.

Not previously published.

TECHNICAL DATA
Size: 109 1/4" (277.5 cm.) x 66" (167.5 cm.).
Technique: slit tapestry; weft-wrap brocaded outlines.
Warp: white wool, 2 Z-yarns S-plied, 9 per in.
Weft: dark brown wool over 2 cords of 4 warps.
Ends: plain weave with brocaded stripes, then warp fringe.
Colors (7): red orange, medium blue, dark blue, blue green, beige, dark brown, white.
Condition: sides show slight wear.

25.
QASHQAI RUG
Iran, 19th century
The Fine Arts Museums of San Francisco.
H. McCoy Jones Collection

The area around the city of Shiraz in southern Iran is inhabited by sedentary Persians living in villages and by a variety of tribes of diverse ethnic origin. Of the latter, the largest group is the Qashqai, a loosely structured confederation of six Turkish subtribes with origins in northwestern Iran. There is also the Khamseh confederacy, an even more complex amalgamation combining five tribes of Arab, Persian, and Turkish origin. The Khamseh existed under the political control of the Qashqai until 1865, when a separate confederacy was established. The nomadic way of life has not disappeared among these various tribal entities, and the Qashqai migrations are the largest in Iran.

The Qashqai, unlike many other tribal groups in Iran, are noted more for their pile weavings than for their flat-weaves. The tribes of the Khamseh weave also, and it is sometimes difficult to distinguish their weavings from those of the Qashqai. This is not surprising in view of their political relationship in the nineteenth century.

This rug is a fine example of the weaving usually assigned to the Qashqai. A traditional field pattern is used, with three and a half diamond-shaped medallions lined up vertically on a dark blue field crammed with small-scale geometric devices, serrated leaves, and wildlife. The popularity of animals in these rugs reminds us of the Qashqai origins in northwestern Iran, a region whose weavings are noted for their use of the same motifs. The field is subdivided into hexagonal areas, each containing a medallion, by characteristic triangular units projecting into the field. The medallions themselves contain a central device common to many rugs of this area—a large hooked medallion seen in a variant form in many Persian rug borders (see, for example, no. 21) as a "turtle" or palmette.

Provenance: ex-collection H. McCoy Jones.

Not previously published.

TECHNICAL DATA
Size: 96¹/₂″ (245 cm.) x 54″ (137 cm.).
Warp: mixed brown wool, 2 Z-yarns S-plied, alternates slightly depressed.
Weft: red wool, 1 Z-yarn, 2 shots.
Pile: wool, 2 Z-yarns, asymmetrical knot open to the left, 10¹/₂ horiz. x 10¹/₂ vert. per in. (110 per sq. in./ 1705 per sq. dm.)
Sides: red and green wool around cable of 4 warps.
Ends: top has narrow plain-weave band, then knotted warp fringe; bottom has warp fringe.
Colors (9): red, red brown, orange, blue (3), green, yellow, white.
Condition: some replaced warp fringe top and bottom; wear into pile at bottom; minor repairs in rug.

26

SOUTH PERSIAN BAG
Iran, Fars Province, probably early 20th century

This charming small bag was intended to be a single pouch, judging by the top finish, and not half of a double-pouched saddlebag designed to be slung over the back of an animal. The addition of tassels, which would have swayed pleasingly, does suggest use on an animal.

Although the piece shows almost no signs of wear, it was probably made in the early years of this century. Identification of a specific origin is very difficult because the patterns seen in small nomadic pieces are ubiquitous throughout Iran and the Caucasus. The main pattern seen here, a series of diamonds containing cross-shaped devices with pointed ends, is a common design, as is the "dazzler" pattern of the tapestry-woven back. These features are often found in the tribal products of the Shiraz area in southern Iran. A bag with this pattern and with similar technical characteristics (although an asymmetrical knot is used) has recently been published with an attribution to the Luri or the Qashqai of this province (Black and Loveless 1979, no. 30). Our bag also has the highly lustrous wool associated with this area.

Provenance: ex-collection Arthur J. Arwine; inherited by present owner in the 1960s.

Not previously published.

TECHNICAL DATA
Size: 14$\frac{1}{2}$″ (37 cm.) x 18$\frac{1}{2}$″ (47 cm.).
Warp: white wool, 2 Z-yarns, alternate warps slightly depressed.
Weft: red wool, single untwisted yarn, 2 shots.
Pile: wool, silk, 2 Z-yarns, symmetrical knot, 11$\frac{1}{2}$ horiz. x 17 vert. per in. (196 per sq. in./ 3038 per sq. dm.).
Sides: varied color wool (in groups) around heavy cord of undetermined construction.
Ends: top has plain weave, with several rows of brocading, folded and sewn; bottom has brocading, braid attached, with tassels.
Colors (13): red, red brown, violet (silk), orange, blue (2), light green (2), dark green, yellow, light brown, black, white.
Condition: woven top end first; one small repair; slight moth damage.

27.

AFSHAR RUG
Iran, 19th century

Due east of Shiraz, in southern Iran, lies the city of Kerman, which has a centuries-old reputation as a rug-weaving center. Like Shiraz, Kerman serves as a marketplace for the various nomadic and now-settled tribes which live in the vicinity. Of the tribes in the area, the best known are the Afshar, a tribe of a Turkish people originally called the Oghuz who started migrating west from Central Asia in the ninth century A.D. Afshar clans settled first in northwestern Iran and then, in the sixteenth and succeeding centuries, in the area to the south and west of Kerman, among other places. Intermixture between the Afshar and the settled Persian population has resulted in a slightly confusing combination of nomadic and urban features in the rugs.

The small rug shown here is of a type usually attributed to the Afshar. Such features as multiple narrow borders, sides overcast in sections of different colors, and ends brocaded in patterns are typical. This rug is an unusually complex and subtle example, however. Similar colors are juxtaposed—gold next to yellow green in the single flowers at the ends of the field, the red next to wine red in the flower calyxes in the diamond lozenges in the field—giving a subtle sculptured effect. The pattern itself, a diamond trellis with four flowers growing into each diamond, is suggestive of a textile pattern. Afshar weavers may have been influenced by the textiles of Kerman, a well-known center for the production of shawls.

Provenance: acquired by present owner in the Washington, D.C., trade around 1970.

Published: Art Institute of Chicago 1973, no. 123.

TECHNICAL DATA
Size: 71 3/4" (182 cm.) x 54 1/4" (137.5 cm.).
Warp: white wool, 2 Z-yarns S-plied, alternates moderately depressed.
Weft: red wool, 1 or occasionally 2 yarns with slight Z twist, 2 shots.
Pile: wool, 1 untwisted yarn, symmetrical knot, 8 horiz. x 13 vert. per in. (104 per sq. in./1612 per sq. dm.).
Sides: colored wool groups (red, blue, blue green, gold, brown) over Z-plied cord of 11 warps.
Ends: band of blue and brown wool brocaded into a diagonal pattern, band of plain weave, then warp fringe, with a few knotted warp groups remaining.
Colors (8): red (2), blue (2), blue green, yellow green, gold, white.
Condition: several small repairs.

28

BROCADED AFSHAR RUG
Iran, 19th century

Many of the nomadic and semi-nomadic peoples of Iran produce a distinctive variety of flat-weave rug, with long and narrow proportions, a field divided into horizontal bands of repeated geometric elements, and generally deep coloring brightened by the selective use of white yarn. These rugs are found in both tapestry and weft-wrap brocade techniques, and are produced by the Baluchi, the Bakhtiyari, the Qashqai, the Kurds of Khurasan, and the Afshar.

The rug shown here, probably woven by the Afshar, belongs to this general type. The horizontal bands in the field are filled with geometric forms paired symmetrically around the central band, a pattern seen in the fields of most of the rugs in this group. The borders, the side and end finish, and the coloring all indicate an identification with the Afshar of the Kerman area. The main border consists of a reciprocal "arrowhead" design, similar to a reciprocal trefoil, in blue and white. This is a border seen in other Afshar pieces, including ones decorated with rows of stylized *botehs*. The ends, with separate rectangular panels outside the border, re-late to many of the Afshar pile rugs, and the sides are festooned with colorful tufts. The coloring is dark overall but not as somber as many of the Baluchi versions. Here the reds and blues are complemented by yellow and light green areas, and particularly by the extensive use of white cotton in both the field and the borders. A broad palette of twelve colors is employed.

Provenance: acquired by present owner in the New York trade around 1970.

Not previously published.

TECHNICAL DATA
Size: 98$\frac{1}{2}$″ (250.5 cm.) x 54$\frac{1}{4}$″ (138 cm.).
Technique: overall weft-wrap brocading.
Warp: white wool, 2 Z-yarns S-plied, 19 per in.
Weft: wool, mostly light orange with some red and pink, 2 Z-yarns S-plied.
Pattern weft: wool, 2 Z-yarns S-plied; cotton, 3 Z-yarns S-plied.
Sides: red orange and green wool around single weft, then 2 cords of 3 wefts; wool tufts of different pattern-weft colors around outer cord.
Ends: warp fringe.
Colors (12): red brown, red orange, dark blue (almost black), medium blue, light blue, dark green, light green, yellow, brown (3), white.
Condition: slight edge wear; a few missing tassels.

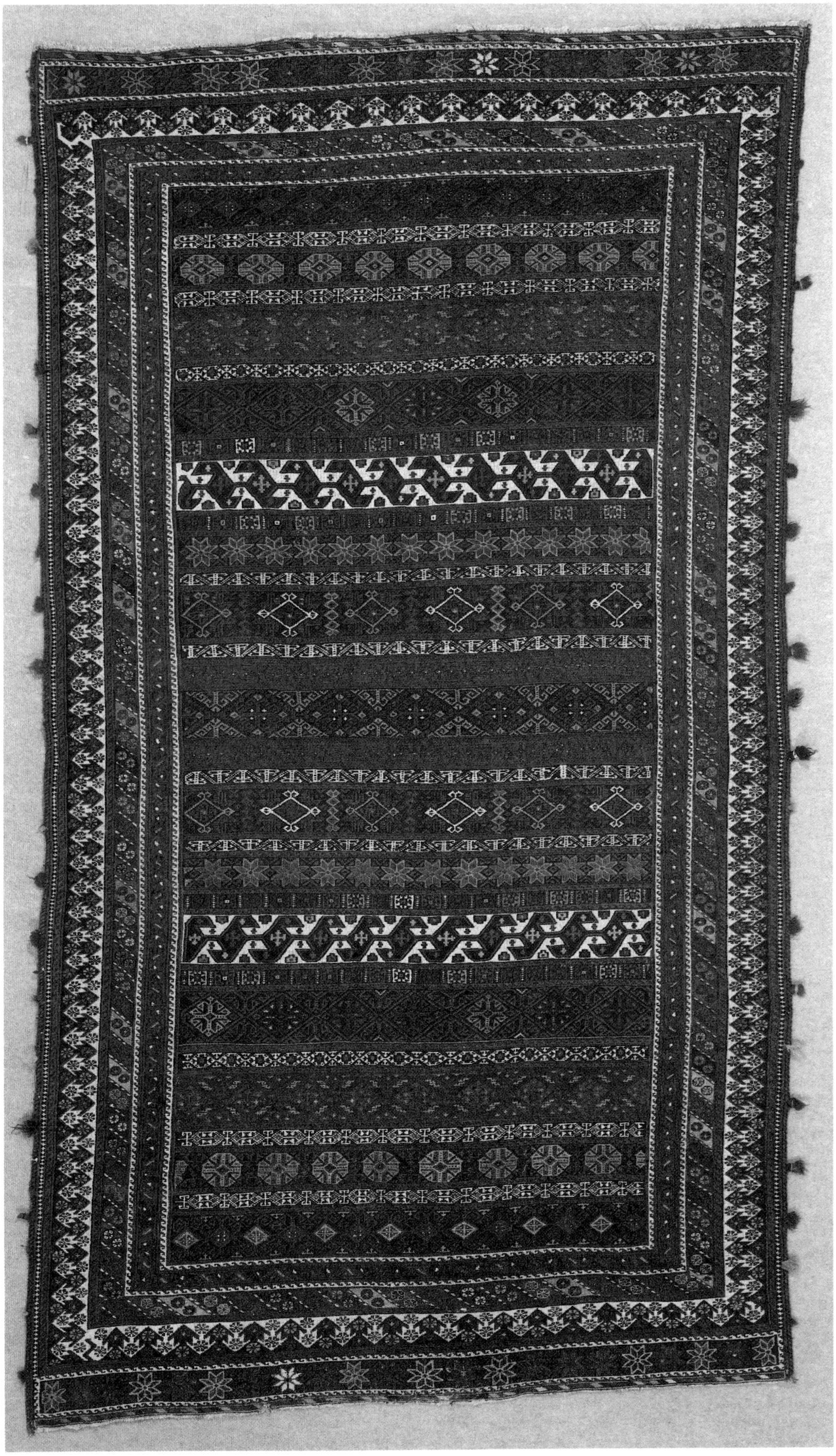

29.

TEKKE RUG

Soviet Turkestan, first half of 19th century
The Fine Arts Museums of San Francisco.
H. McCoy Jones Collection

The rugs produced by the various Turko-man tribes of Soviet Turkestan, Afghan-istan, and northeastern Iran make up a virtually unmistakable group. The seemingly monochromatic use of red and the repeating patterns of geometric forms, many resembling medallions, are common denominators of the rugs of this area.

The Turkomans are a Turkish people who started moving westward out of Central Asia in the ninth cen-tury A.D., reaching places as distant as Anatolia. There is evidence that the Turkomans had an impact on rug weaving in Anatolia and Persia, but only in Turkestan did tribes maintain their own identities until relatively recent times. Only here are we able to see Turkoman products which are heir to the original tribal traditions, more or less unaffected by court or commercial inter-ests or by intermixture with the traditions of sedentary populations.

Of the twenty-four Turkoman tribes named by early historians, several still existed in recent times. The Tekke were the largest tribal entity in the nineteenth century, and they, like the other Turkoman peoples, produced a full range of weavings, most of them with a knotted-pile construction. Such weavings were strictly functional in nature. They provided the nomads with furniture, covers, and storage containers for use in camp, when the circular tents were set up, or for use when on the move.

The rug shown here is known as a main rug. It was reserved for special occasions, being unrolled on felts at the back of the tent where the host would greet his guests. Because of the dimensions of the tents, main rugs are always about this size. Main rugs were tradi-tionally decorated with repeated rows of a geometric device called a *gul* ("flower") in Persian or Turkish. Specific *gul* designs are seemingly favored by particular tribes. Both the octagonal main *gul* and the cross-shaped secondary *guls* seen on this superb rug are usu-ally found on pieces woven by the Tekke.

Provenance: ex-collection H. McCoy Jones, who acquired the rug in the mid-1920s in Odessa.

Published: Textile Museum 1963, no. 48; Jones and Boucher 1973, no. 1.

TECHNICAL DATA
Size: 93¼" (237 cm.) x 74¾" (190 cm.) excluding skirts totaling 21" (53 cm.).
Warp: off-white wool, 2 Z-yarns S-plied, warps even.
Weft: off-white wool, 2 Z-yarns, 2 shots.
Pile: wool, 2 Z-yarns S-plied, asymmetrical knot open to the right (last row on both sides is symmetrical), 10 horiz. x 16 vert. per in. (160 per sq. in./2480 per sq. dm.).
Sides: dark blue wool around 3 pairs of warps.
Ends: plain weave, knotted warp fringe.
Colors (6): mahogany red, orange red, dark blue, medium blue, brown, white.
Condition: excellent.

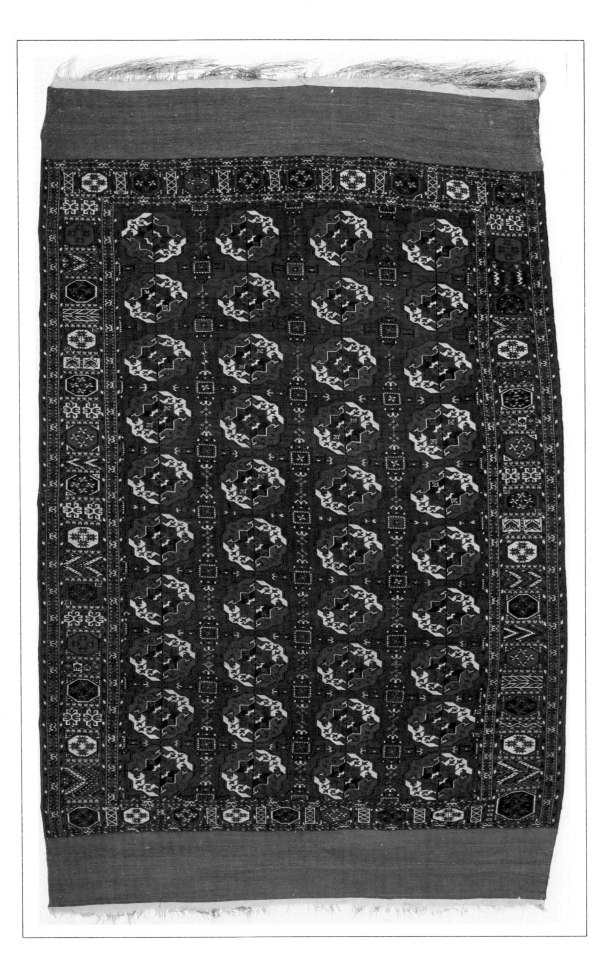

30

TEKKE STORAGE-BAG PANEL
Soviet Turkestan, second half of 19th century
The Textile Museum, Washington, D.C.
Gift of John W. Irvine, Jr.

Around the insides of the circular Turkoman tents were placed a variety of rectangular bags of different sizes. In these were kept clothing and household items. Such bags were attached to the wooden framework which supported the felt walls and roof of the structure.

The piece shown here is the front panel from a *chuval*, a storage bag of large size. Although the use of the *gul* was generally restricted to main rugs, certain tribes used them on large storage-bag panels as well. The *gul* seen here, with its flattened octagonal shape and turreted projections on interior and exterior, is traditionally associated with the Salor tribe, but it is found on Saryk and Tekke bags as well. The technical features of this piece (asymmetric knot open to the right, the use of magenta silk only inside the turrets) and the quality of the wool suggest a Tekke origin. An unusual design feature is the appearance of large *gul* halves along the top and bottom edges of the field, where the secondary *gul* element is usually repeated.

The significance of the *gul* designs to the Turkoman tribes has not been firmly established. Moshkova (1980, pp. 20–21) views the *guls* as totemic, representing with varying degrees of degeneration the original tribal symbols. They belonged exclusively to one tribe and fell from use only when that tribe was defeated by another. At that point, according to Moshkova, the *gul* of the defeated tribe became a "dead" *gul* and was used only on small pieces and not on the main rugs. A different view is held by Cammann (1972, p. 49), who sees no heraldic significance in terms of tribal identification but agrees that particular forms were favored by particular tribes. In either case, because of the movements of tribes in the nineteenth century, it becomes increasingly difficult to identify tribal origin strictly by *gul* design. Technical characteristics have therefore assumed an increasingly important role in the grouping of Turkoman rugs.

Provenance: ex-collection John W. Irvine, Jr.

Published: Reed 1966, no. 3; Jones and Boucher 1973, no. 21; and Denny 1979, colorplate 21.

TECHNICAL DATA

Size: 29 1/4" (74.5 cm.) x 43 3/4" (111 cm.).

Warp: ivory wool, 2 Z-yarns S-plied, alternate warps slightly depressed.

Weft: brown wool, 2 Z-yarns S-plied, 1 shot.

Pile: wool, 2 Z-yarns S-plied, and silk, single untwisted yarn, asymmetrical knot open to the right, 12 1/2 horiz. x 24 vert. per in. (300 per sq. in./4650 per sq. dm.).

Sides: not original.

Ends: top (by weave) has plain weave, folded and sewn under; bottom has plain weave, then warp fringe.

Colors (9): red, orange, magenta (silk), dark blue, light blue, green, yellow, brown, white.

Condition: woven top end first; a few small repairs along top edge.

31

TEKKE STORAGE-BAG PANEL
Soviet Turkestan, second half of 19th century

TEKKE STORAGE-BAG PANEL
Soviet Turkestan, 19th century

Certain storage-bag panels woven by the Tekke and other tribes have a pattern of narrow horizontal bands of repeated geometric elements across an otherwise plain field, often with a wide end band. Some of these are completely pile-woven, while others, such as this example (no. 31), have knotted decorated bands on a plain-weave ground. The broad end band of this piece is decorated with a treelike pattern which is brightened by the use of white cotton for the ground. The nature of the patterns employed in decorating these pieces has resulted in considerable confusion regarding tribal origin, but technical characteristics all argue for a Tekke attribution. A similar piece is in the Metropolitan Museum of Art (acc. no. 22.100.32; Mackie and Thompson 1980, no. 33).

Another type of Turkoman storage bag is the *torba*, similar in width to nos. 30 and 31, but shallower. This lovely Tekke *torba* panel (no. 32) has a characteristic pattern made up of minor *guls* popular in the Tekke vocabulary, one as a primary *gul* and one as a secondary device. Although the basic color of most Turkoman pieces is red, the supplementary colors employed have a major effect on the overall tonality—in the case of no. 32 a decided orange cast. A subtle rhythm is established here through the use of different colors in the *gul* quadrants.

31.

Provenance: acquired by present owner in the California trade in 1978.

Not previously published.

TECHNICAL DATA
Size: 29″ (73.5 cm.) x 50¾″ (129 cm.).
Warp: white wool, 2 Z-yarns S-plied, warps even.
Weft: white, red wool, 2 Z-yarns, 2 shots.
Pile: wool and cotton, 2 Z-yarns S-plied, asymmetrical knot open to the right (last row on both sides is symmetrical), 12 horiz. x 36 vert. per in. (432 per sq. in./6696 per sq. dm.).
Sides: red wool and white cotton around 2 warps.
Ends: top has plain weave, folded and sewn, braided cord attached; bottom has plain weave.
Colors (6): red, magenta, orange, yellow, black, white (cotton).
Condition: minor repairs to edges; worn into pile at bottom.

32.

Provenance: acquired by present owner in the New Jersey trade in the 1960s.

Not previously published.

TECHNICAL DATA
Size: 16¼″ (41 cm.) x 50½″ (128 cm.).
Warp: white wool, 2 Z-yarns S-plied, warps even.
Weft: mixed brown and white wool, 2 Z-yarns S-plied, 2 shots.
Pile: wool, 2 Z-yarns S-plied, asymmetrical knot open to the right, 11 horiz. x 22 vert. per in. (242 per sq. in./3751 per sq. dm.).
Sides: reddish orange wool around 2 pairs of 2 warps.
Ends: top has plain weave, folded and sewn; bottom has trace of plain weave, then warp fringe.
Colors (7): red, orange, dark blue, light blue, dark green, dark brown, white.
Condition: a few stains; dark brown and green corroded.

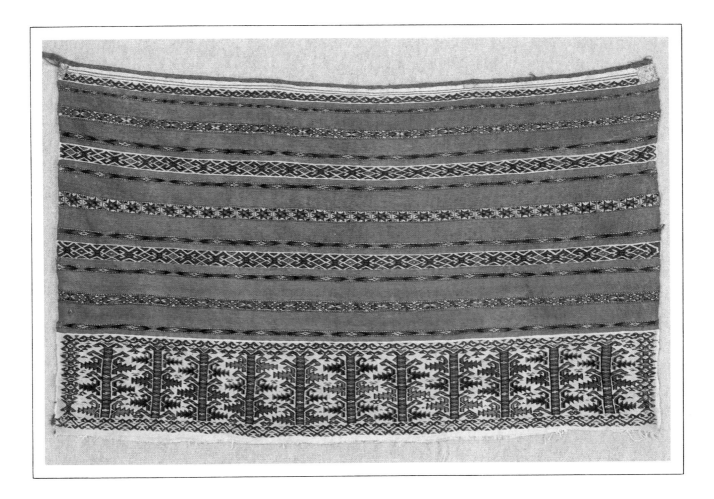

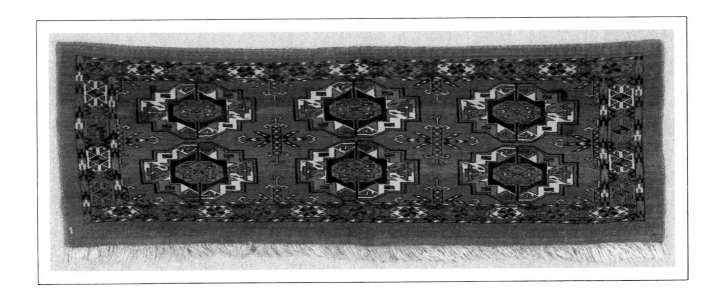

33.

SMALL TEKKE BAG PANEL
Soviet Turkestan, mid-19th century

Small bags for personal possessions were woven by the Tekke with front panels bearing a characteristic pattern. This normally consists of two or three white-ground squares containing treelike motifs related to the wide panel decoration of the Tekke storage-bag panel (no. 31). The treelike design on the small bag shown here is placed symmetrically along the central horizontal axis; others extend to the full height of the panels. These small bags, known as *mafrash*, are more common with three squares than with two. This example has a particularly rich range of materials, with the ground of the squares worked in a brilliant white cotton and various highlights of magenta silk used in the field. A very similar example is published by Mackie and Thompson (1980, no. 39), who assign all of these pieces to the middle third of the nineteenth century. Some extant examples of these small bags still have the cord attached to both sides for hanging as well as colorful fringes across the bottom (see Azadi 1975, no. 44).

Provenance: acquired by present owner from an antique furniture dealer in New York in 1977.

Not previously published.

TECHNICAL DATA
Size: 11$\frac{1}{2}$" (29 cm.) × 28$\frac{3}{4}$" (73 cm.).
Warp: white wool, 2 Z-yarns S-plied, alternates slightly depressed.
Weft: brown wool, mostly single yarns with slight Z-twist, but a few 2 Z-yarns S-plied, 2 shots.
Pile: wool, 2 Z-yarns S-plied; cotton, 2 Z-yarns S-plied; silk, single untwisted yarn; asymmetrical knot open to the right, 11 horiz. × 22 vert. per in. (242 per sq. in./3751 per sq. dm.).
Sides: not original.
Ends: warp fringe.
Colors (8): red, orange, magenta (silk), blue, green, yellow, brown, white (cotton).
Condition: sides and ends worn, fraying.

34

TEKKE CAMEL DECORATION
Soviet Turkestan, early 19th century
The Fine Arts Museums of San Francisco.
H. McCoy Jones Collection

This well-known weaving is one of a group of pentagonal pieces used in pairs to decorate the sides of a camel in the wedding procession. It would have been embellished with strings of multiple tassels hanging from the bottom and sides, similar to those on no. 39. Such *asmalyk,* as they are called, were made in pairs.

The dating of Turkoman rugs is a tricky business, and the opinions of specialists and collectors vary widely. These views include the conservative position taken by Joseph McMullan that no existing Turkoman pieces predate 1850, because of the hard wear they receive. On the other hand, Siawosch Azadi holds that some examples have survived from the seventeenth century. Both of these positions seem extreme, and an early nineteenth-century date for this piece can be justified.

The principal reason for such a dating is the clarity of the design, which has degenerated far less than most Turkoman designs we are familiar with. The field pattern consists of a diamond lattice, each compartment containing a blue-and-white bird perched on a stem with diagonal branches. Above the bird are two serrated leaves, one blue and one white. The main border consists of a scrolling vine with curling, serrated leaves in red on a white ground. It has been suggested by Moshkova that *gul* designs were originally based on the bird totems of various tribes (1980, pp. 24–25). If birds really were part of the original *gul* designs, this is one of the few instances where an archaic design has been preserved.

Pentagonal camel decorations used to be assigned exclusively to the Yomut. McCoy Jones has published this piece as the work of the Yomut, who do in fact produce most of the pieces woven in this pentagonal shape. But in a recent article (1980) Robert Pinner and Michael Franses, following work by Jon Thompson and Siawosch Azadi, present very convincing arguments for a Tekke origin for this group. Some of the reasons are technical and deal with the knotting, the quality of the wool, and the coloration. Others are stylistic and deal with the fact that the border pattern, heretofore associated exclusively with the Yomut, is found in the end panels of two Tekke main-rug fragments.

The most closely related *asmalyk,* formerly in the collection of Arthur Jenkins and now in the Textile Museum, was published by Mackie and Thompson (1980, no. 43).

Provenance: ex-collections Fred Harvey, H. McCoy Jones. Acquired by Harvey in Tehran for about $60 in 1931 (see his *Hali* article).

Published: Schürmann 1969, no. 34; Jones 1970, no. 28; Jones and Boucher 1976, no. 34; Pinner and Franses 1980a, fig. 225; Harvey 1981, no. 1.

TECHNICAL DATA
Size: 31″ (79 cm.) × 47½″ (121 cm.).
Warp: white wool, 2 Z-yarns S-plied, warps even.
Weft: natural medium brown to gray wool, 2 Z-yarns with slight S-ply, 2 shots (4 in one place).
Pile: wool, 2 Z-yarns, asymmetrical knot open to right (last 2 rows on each side have an odd knot—an asymmetrical knot open to the right, with an extra wrap around the right warp), 12 horiz. × 19 vert. per in. (228 per sq. in./3534 per sq. dm.).
Sides: red wool around 2 cords of 2 warps.
Ends: top has plain weave, folded and sewn, 5 mounting loops attached; bottom has warp fringe.
Colors (7): red, orange, dark blue, blue green, yellow (off-white on front), brown, white.
Condition: a few small areas of reknotting and repair, especially on sides.

35.

TEKKE CAMEL DECORATION
Soviet Turkestan, first half of 19th century
W. Parsons Todd Foundation,
Macculloch Hall Historical Museum, Morristown, N.J.

This charming piece is thought to be a camel decoration, but the specific placement on the camel is uncertain. Most likely it decorated the bride's litter on top of the camel during the wedding procession. Moshkova (1980, p. 23) mentioned a piece which decorated the chest of the camel in the wedding procession, another possibility for this type. With the two hanging flaps and fringe at the sides, pieces such as this are similar in format to the door surrounds woven by several tribes, but they are too small to have served such a purpose.

Azadi (1975, no. 47) claims that the shape is very rare and that the Tekke stopped weaving these pieces in the eighteenth century, a date which seems too early. Mackie and Thompson (1980, no. 42) published an example very similar to this one in the Textile Museum.

Franses and Pinner (1980, p. 202) list twenty-two Tekke examples of this design.

Provenance: ex-collection W. Parsons Todd.

Published: Thacher 1940, no. 17.

TECHNICAL DATA
Size: 21¼″ (54 cm.) × 30¾″ (78 cm.).
Warp: white wool, 2 Z-yarns S-plied, alternates slightly depressed.
Weft: brown wool, 2 Z-yarns S-plied, 2 shots.
Pile: wool, 2 Z-yarns S-plied, asymmetrical knot open to the right (last two on each side are symmetrical), 11 horiz. × 20 vert. per in. (220 per sq. in./3410 per sq. dm.).
Sides: blue, red wool around 2 warps, braided cord attached to upper part.
Ends: top has plain weave, folded and sewn; bottom has plain weave, folded and sewn, fringe added.
Colors (6): red, orange, dark blue, yellow, dark brown, white.
Condition: woven top end first; rejoined split where left flap meets horizontal part.

36.

YOMUT RUG

Soviet Turkestan, first half of 19th century
The Metropolitan Museum of Art, New York City.
Gift of Dr. and Mrs. F. M. Al Akl, 1961

The most diverse assortment of Turkoman weavings are assigned to the Yomut, a tribe of unknown origin which is mentioned by historians as existing in the Khurasan area in the sixteenth century. The variety of these weavings suggests several tribal origins, but until more can be determined about these tribes the general Yomut classification will be retained. In the nineteenth century, the period from which most extant Yomut pieces date, the tribe occupied two areas, near the city of Khiva along the northern reaches of the Oxus River and along the southeastern shores of the Caspian Sea, extending into present-day Iran.

Main rugs of the Yomut are found with a variety of *gul* designs. Certain *guls* appear with secondary devices, repeated across the field in horizontal and vertical rows as in the Tekke main rug included here (no. 29). Others, however, appear without secondary motifs and are arranged in offset rows.

This fine example of a Yomut main rug has a characteristic *gul* consisting of a series of graduated vertical panels, with serrated ends and alternating color, grouped around a central hexagon. The panels contain little anchor-like plants. The field pattern in this rug is organized into diagonal rows through the use of color. The color scheme is particularly harmonious and rich, with the green and two blues of the *guls* placed against the deep mahogany ground. Two unusual features are the designs of the main border and the end skirts. The main border has a repeating pattern of hexagons containing palmette-like devices, not one of the standard borders, while the end skirts have five offset rows of small floral units organized by color into a striking pattern of diamonds and X's.

Provenance: ex-collection Dr. and Mrs. F. M. Al Akl.

Published: Thacher 1940, no. 20; Dimand 1961, no. 26; Dimand and Mailey 1973, no. 188.

TECHNICAL DATA
Size: 108½″ (275.5 cm.) x 63¾″ (162 cm.).
Warp: white wool, 2 Z-yarns S-plied, warps even.
Weft: dark brown wool, 2 Z-yarns S-plied, 2 shots.
Pile: wool, 2 Z-yarns S-plied, symmetrical knot, 9 horiz. x 13 vert. per in. (117 per sq. in./1813 per sq. dm.).
Sides: not original.
Ends: warp fringe.
Colors (9): red, red brown, purple, light blue, dark blue, green, yellow, dark brown, white.
Condition: half of right outer guard replaced; several patched or rewoven areas in field.

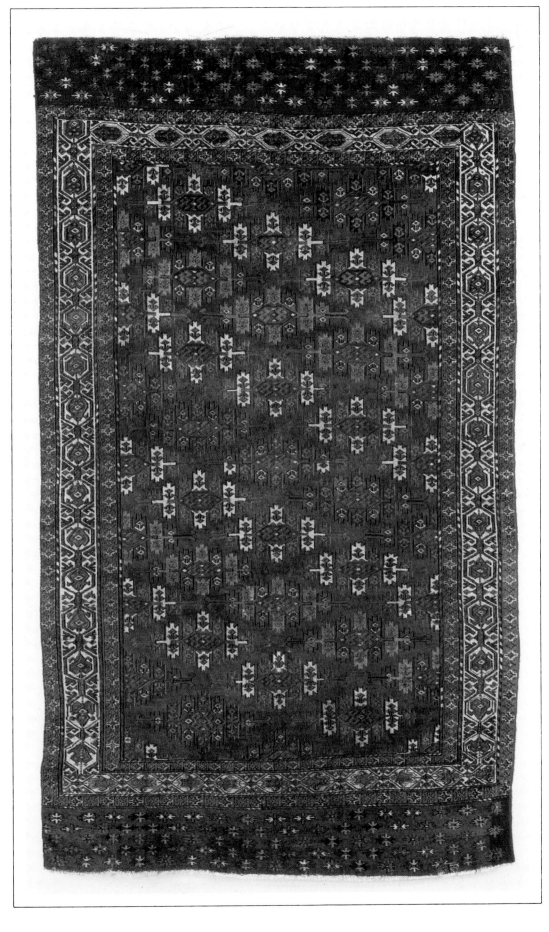

37

YOMUT RUG
Soviet Turkestan, early 19th century

This outstanding main rug has two *gul* types seen on Yomut weavings. The main *gul* is a flattened octagon containing four pairs of animals. Moshkova considers these to be birds, consistent with her theories regarding the use of the tribal totems in these emblems (see discussion for no. 34). She describes (1980, pp. 24–25) the likely evolution of these H-shaped bird forms by citing a rug in which the counterparts to these devices lack the horizontal connector. The form seen on our rug, and in most other examples of this *gul*, probably derives then from a pair of birds. Such *guls* are called *tauk-nuska*, or "figure of a hen," by the tribe which uses this device as its tribal pattern, according to Moshkova.

The secondary *gul* is a diamond with projecting hooks. Secondary *guls* are offset from the rows of main *guls* and form a diagonal pattern of their own, based on coloring. The main *guls* have color alternation of their central, cross-shaped devices, resulting also in a diagonal row arrangement. The main border is the classic Yomut "boat" border, whose evolution from an earlier flower-and-palmette design Thompson has discussed (Mackie and Thompson 1980, p. 152, fig. 46). It is likely that at one time this rug had long skirts at the ends.

While it is true that the primary *gul* seen in this rug is often employed by the Arabatchi and the Ersari, particularly a subtribe called the Kizil Ayak, other design elements such as the secondary *gul* and the border design are typical of Yomut products. Technical characteristics, particularly the use of the symmetrical knot, clearly indicate a Yomut origin.

Not previously published.

TECHNICAL DATA

Size: 94¼″ (242 cm.) x 62¼″ (158 cm.).
Warp: mixed brown wool, 2 Z-yarns S-plied, warps even.
Weft: brown wool, 2 Z-yarns S-plied, 2 shots.
Pile: wool, 2 Z-yarns, symmetrical knot, 9 horiz. x 17 vert. per in. (153 per sq. in./2371 per sq. dm.).
Sides: replaced overcasting, around traces of original blue wool, over 2 cords of 2 warps.
Ends: warp fringe.
Colors (6): red brown, orange, dark blue, green, dark brown, white.
Condition: somewhat uneven wear; various small repairs and reknotted areas.

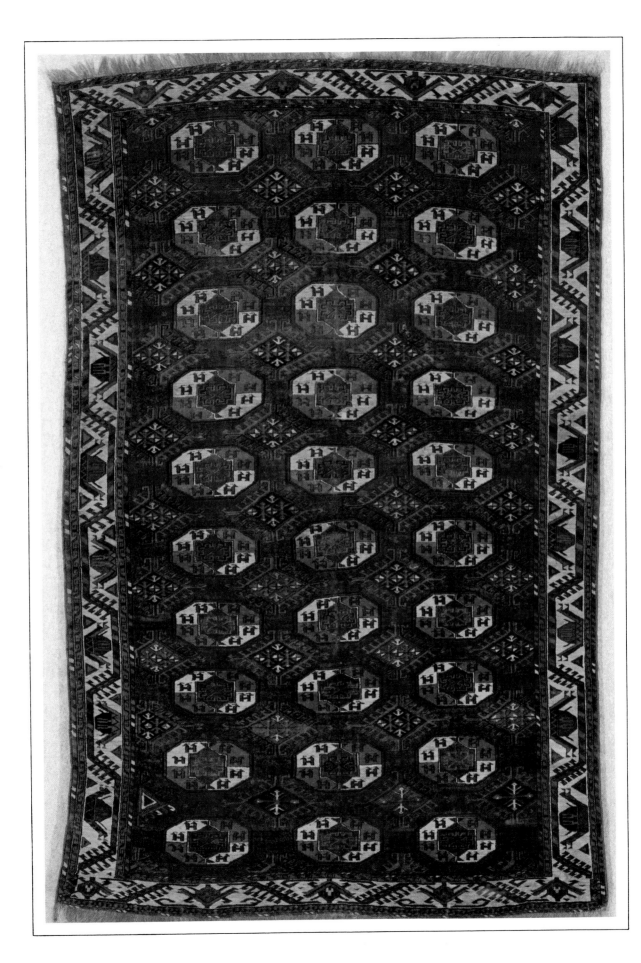

38.

YOMUT DOORWAY RUG
Soviet Turkestan, mid-19th century

The doorway rugs, or *engsi*, of the Saryk, Tekke, Yomut, and Ersari tribes are all well known to specialists and collectors. Such rugs were hung on special occasions on the outside of the door frame of the tent, pile facing out (see Andrews 1980, p. 56). Loops for hanging exist on the top corners of many of these rugs (see no. 43).

Doorway rugs have certain design characteristics which single them out. The field pattern is organized into quarters through the placement of horizontal and vertical bands which intersect near the center of the field. Cammann suggests that the Four Gardens of Paradise are represented (see entry no. 20 and Cammann 1972, p. 19). The quadrants of the field are decorated with offset rows of small geometric devices. At the bottom of the rug is usually a wide panel or two, filled with repeating patterns of various secondary motifs.

This rug is a Yomut version of the type. It has lively coloring, with an emphasis on blue and orange, and much white is employed for highlights. A whole range of minor patterns and devices seen on Yomut weavings is present here—the small "plant" designs of the field; the serrated, curled leaves of the side borders; the geometric devices in the first panel below the field, reminiscent of the *gul* of no. 36; and the "tree" design of the bottom panel.

Provenance: acquired by present owner in the New York trade in 1975.

Not previously published.

TECHNICAL DATA
Size: 71″ (180 cm.) x 50½″ (128.5 cm.).
Warp: white (and some brown) wool, 2 Z-yarns S-plied, alternates range from slight to moderate depression.
Weft: dark brown, occasionally orange or light brown, wool, 2 Z-yarns S-plied, 2 shots.
Pile: wool, 2 Z-yarns S-plied, symmetrical knot, 8½ horiz. x 15 vert. per in. (127½ per sq. in./1976 per sq. dm.).
Sides: blue and orange, grouped, around 4 pairs of warps.
Ends: plain weave, brocaded stripes, then warp fringe.
Colors (8): red, red brown, orange, medium blue, dark blue (black), green, dark brown, white.
Condition: minor repairs on edges, one in field.

39

YOMUT CAMEL DECORATION
Soviet Turkestan, second half of 19th century

Yomut camel decorations with this type of design are not uncommon, but it is unusual to find one in such pristine condition, with all of its tassels and hanging cords intact. Like the Tekke example included here (no. 34), this piece was one of a pair of decorations attached to the sides of the bride's camel in the wedding procession. The field pattern is the common Yomut "tree" design, seen also on the bottom skirt of the Yomut doorway rug (no. 38). The pattern is divided into five vertical panels with alternating coloration.

A very similar example is pictured by Bogolyubov (1973, pl. 19), who assigns it to the Ogurjali, a sedentary people living in houses on the southeastern coast of the Caspian and on nearby islands. He describes them as a non-Salor subtribe, but they are usually considered

Yomut. The weavings of the Ogurjali have not yet been isolated.

Provenance: ex-collection Arthur J. Arwine.

Not previously published.

TECHNICAL DATA
Size: 50¹/₂″ (128 cm.) x 34¹/₂″ (88 cm.).
Warp: white wool, 2 Z-yarns S-plied, alternates slightly to moderately depressed.
Weft: brown wool, single yarn with slight Z twist, 2 shots.
Pile: wool, 2 Z-yarns S-plied, symmetrical knot, 10 horiz. x 19 vert. per in. (190 per sq. in./2945 per sq. dm.).
Sides: blue green wool around cord of 3 warps, tassels attached.
Ends: plain weave, brocaded, folded, and sewn under. Top has 3 braided cords attached for hanging. Bottom has cord attached from which hang the tassel cords and tassels.
Colors (9): rust red, wine red, light orange, medium blue, dark blue, dark green, medium brown, dark brown, white.
Condition: excellent.

40.

CHODOR BAG PANEL
Soviet Turkestan, second half of 19th century
The Textile Museum, Washington, D.C.
Gift of John W. Irvine, Jr.

41.

TURKOMAN CAMEL TRAPPING
Soviet Turkestan, first half of 19th century

The Chodor is another tribe noted for its weaving in the eighteenth and nineteenth centuries. Originally considered by Bogolyubov to be part of the Yomut tribe, it has long since been recognized as a separate entity. Chodor rugs employ the Persian knot open to the right, like most Tekke and a small percentage of Yomut rugs, but certain other features distinguish them. The coloring tends to be on the dark side, with a pronounced purplish cast. Main rugs usually bear rows of either the *tauk-nuska gul*—the flattened octagonal *gul* with pairs of birds in each quadrant—or a type specifically associated with the Chodor.

The latter *gul*, a step-sided polygon with hooks at the top and bottom, is also found on Chodor bag panels such as the one shown here (no. 40), divided in half along the top and bottom edges of the field. In this example, each half-*gul* contains a central stem flanked by little groups of squares. These squares are seen in some, presumably earlier, pieces with bird heads projecting out, suggesting that the devices on this rug may be stylized renderings of yet another tribal device that incorporated birds in the design.

This cheerfully colored panel (no. 41) seems too wide to have functioned as a shallow wall bag and may have served as a camel trapping. Distinctive features are the coloring, which contrasts intense blues, orange, and pink (used in the centers of the secondary *guls*) with a red brown ground, and the deep, lustrous wool. The design consists of four rows of three flattened octagons, alternating with offset rows of secondary *guls* with radial arms. Alternating colors are used in this panel throughout the main and the secondary *guls*.

A minor but interesting design feature is the use of the triangular forms between the secondary *guls*. From each of these hang strings of two or three beads. Related devices can be seen hanging from the tips of the serrated "tree" branches in the skirt of the Yomut doorway rug

(no. 38). Perhaps there is an amuletic function for this device, a possibility noted for a similar motif found on an Anatolian piece (no. 8).

The attribution of this piece is uncertain. The trapping belongs to a small group of weavings isolated by Jon Thompson (Mackie and Thompson 1980, pp. 135–44) which employ the asymmetrical knot open to the left and have characteristic coloring, particularly a "pink-yellow" (described here as light orange) and a cochineal color (here pink), seen in the secondary *guls*. Thompson links the group, including a piece (no. 59) very similar to this example, to the Imreli tribe, with whom no weavings have specifically been connected. Evidence for this association seems slight, and a firm attribution cannot yet be made.

40.

Provenance: ex-collections Arthur Urbane Dilley, John W. Irvine, Jr. Acquired by Irvine at a private Hajji Baba Club auction of some of Dilley's rugs.

Not previously published.

TECHNICAL DATA
Size: 12″ (30 cm.) x 35″ (89 cm.).
Warp: ivory wool, 2 Z-yarns S-plied, alternates slightly depressed.
Weft: reddish brown wool, 2 Z-yarns S-plied, 2 shots.
Pile: wool, 2 Z-yarns S-plied, asymmetrical knot open to the right, 9 horiz. x 20 vert. per in. (180 per sq. in./2790 per sq. dm.).
Sides: not original.
Ends: top is not original; bottom has warp fringe.
Colors (7): red (2), dark blue, dark green, yellow, brown, ivory.
Condition: repairs to edges, 3 with later overcasting.

41.

Not previously published.

TECHNICAL DATA
Size: 58¼″ (148 cm.) x 22¼″ (56.5 cm.).
Warp: white wool, 2 Z-yarns S-plied, alternates slightly depressed.
Weft: white to medium brown wool, 2 Z-yarns S-plied, 2 shots.
Pile: wool, 3 (some 2) Z-yarns, asymmetrical knot open to the left, 9½ horiz. x 18 vert. per in. (171 per sq. in./2650 per sq. dm.).
Sides: not original.
Ends: not original.
Colors (8): red brown, pink, light orange, orange, dark blue, medium blue, dark brown, white.
Condition: several repaired slits at top and bottom; pink corroded.

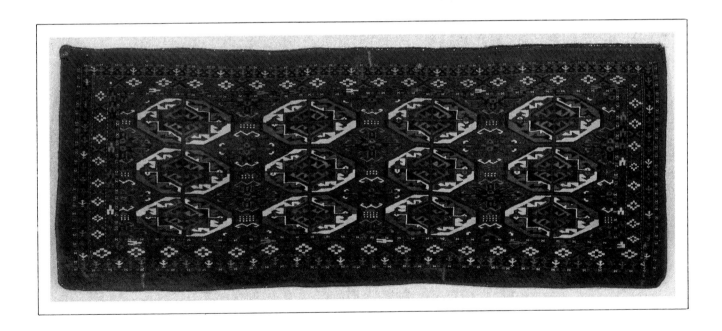

42

SMALL TURKOMAN RUG
Soviet Turkestan, late 19th century

Small rugs have no prescribed place in the standard litany of Turkoman woven furniture or accessories, although examples are known from most tribes. They must be floor coverings, since no other function is apparent, and they share the secondary status of bags and similar pieces, not bearing main tribal *guls.* Azadi (1975, no. 38) shows a small Ersari rug with an unusual pattern of starlike motifs, while Mackie and Thompson (1980, no. 29) illustrate a Tekke with two secondary *guls* repeated in a more conventional manner. Like the Ersari, our piece has a field pattern made up of non-*gul* motifs, motifs which are likely to be found embellishing the end panels of storage bags, doorway rugs, or main rugs. These are small stepped diamonds arranged in vertical, offset rows of diamond compartments.

The attribution of this piece is problematic. Previous publications, listed below, have assigned it to the Chodor, an attribution with certain merits. Although this precise skirt motif is not known to me in other examples, the arrangement of the little hooked devices in a chevron pattern, based on their color, is a popular Chodor convention. Asymmetric knots open to the right are seen in Tekke, Ersari, and some Yomut pieces, as well as in Chodor ones. Against a Chodor attribution is the coloring, which lacks the purple or aubergine so common in Chodor weavings. Speaking for a Tekke attribution are the coloring, the use of a symmetrical knot at the edges, and the soft but substantial feel of the wool. Arguing against any specific attribution, however, is the use of a dyed light orange or pink weft, usually in a single pass between rows of knots. This rug may well be a late nineteenth-century product, a fusion of weaving traditions mirroring the breakdown of tribal integrity taking place at that time.

Provenance: ex-collection Amos B. Thacher.

Published: Thacher 1940, pl. 32; Dimand 1961, no. 28.

TECHNICAL DATA
Size: 40″ (101.5 cm.) x 35¾″ (91 cm.).
Warp: white wool, 2 Z-yarns S-plied, alternates slightly depressed.
Weft: light orange wool, 2 Z-yarns S-plied, 1 or occasionally 2 shots.
Pile: wool, 2 Z-yarns, asymmetrical knot open to the right (last 3 rows on each side are symmetrical), 10 horiz. x 19 vert. per in. (190 per sq. in./2945 per sq. dm.).
Sides: blue wool around 2 warps.
Ends: top has plain weave, then warp fringe; bottom has plain weave with brocaded pattern at end, then knotted warp fringe.
Colors (8): wine red, reddish brown, orange, green, yellow, dark brown, black, white.
Condition: 3 patches in border or edge of field; several minor repairs; wefts loose along bottom.

43

ERSARI DOORWAY RUG
Soviet Turkestan or Afghanistan, 19th century

The Ersari are an enormous tribe made up of many subtribes spread over an area ranging from Soviet Turkestan around the city of Bukhara, south into Afghanistan. They are best known for their large rugs employing rows of the characteristic large rounded *guls*. These are the rugs often called Afghans, which has significance in a geographic, but not an ethnographic, sense. The range of Ersari weavings is broad, but most are coarsely woven and somewhat somber in coloring. The foundation fiber is frequently all brown goat hair.

This Ersari doorway rug is a fine example of the type. It is gayer in coloring than many, the reddish brown ground color brightened considerably by the use of white, mainly in the borders, pink, and a medium blue. The field is organized into quadrants, similar to the Yomut rug discussed earlier (no. 38), but here the vertical element in the field consists of two arched elements, one above the other. The presence of these forms and the existence of pointed arches along the tops of related Tekke, Saryk, and other Ersari pieces have led specialists to call all of these rugs prayer rugs, although there is no evidence that they were ever put to such use. This example still has the hanging loops at the upper corners. These are part of the end finish of the rug.

Provenance: acquired by present owner in the New York trade in the 1960s.

Published: Reed 1966, no. 46.

TECHNICAL DATA
Size: 69″ (175 cm.) x 55½″ (141 cm.).
Warp: mixed brown wool, 2 Z-yarns S-plied, warps even.
Weft: brown wool, 2 Z-yarns S-plied, 2 shots.
Pile: wool, 2 Z-yarns S-plied, asymmetrical knot open to the right, 7 horiz. x 9 vert. per in. (63 per sq. in./976 per sq. dm.).
Sides: brown wool around 3 sets of 3 warps.
Ends: top has plain weave, with brocaded stripes which extend into braided loops at corners, folded and sewn under; bottom has plain weave with brocaded stripes, warp fringe.
Colors (7): red, pink, medium blue, dark blue, yellow, brown, ivory.
Condition: excellent.

44.
ERSARI BAG PANEL
Soviet Turkestan, 19th century

A distinctive type of Ersari product is quite different in appearance from the *engsi*, or doorway rug (no. 43), and from the larger rugs bearing the tribal *gul* patterns. These are rugs whose designs are not tribal in appearance but which closely resemble the resist-dyed *ikat* textiles produced in the emirate of Bukhara. Such a rug is shown here. It is a panel from a large bag and it repeats, in a much more angular fashion, the floral designs seen on textiles. Alternation of colors in the rug results in a secondary diagonal emphasis, as seen in other Turkoman pieces.

Together with many larger rugs which seem to draw heavily from Persian sources for their designs, these pieces are sometimes called Beshir rugs. They have a lighter palette than most Ersari pieces because of the extensive use of yellow and green. There is a town called Beshir in which rugs of this floral group are produced (König 1980, p. 201), so the name is perhaps appropriate. At any rate, it is useful for identifying the group as long as it is not used to mean all Ersari weaving.

Provenance: acquired by present owner in the New York trade in the 1960s.

Not previously published.

TECHNICAL DATA
Size: 41³/₄″ (106 cm.) x 66¹/₂″ (169 cm.).
Warp: light brown wool, 2 Z-yarns S-plied, warps even.
Weft: light brown wool, 2 Z-yarns, 2 shots.
Pile: wool, 2 Z-yarns S-plied, asymmetrical knot open to the right, 7 horiz. x 12 vert. per in. (84 per sq. in./1302 per sq. dm.).
Sides: dark brown wool around 2 pairs of 2 warps.
Ends: top has plain weave with brocaded stripe, folded and sewn under; bottom has plain weave, folded and sewn under.
Colors (7): red, orange, blue, green, yellow, brown, ivory.
Condition: small repairs at edges.

45.
FRAGMENT OF A COMPARTMENT RUG
India, 17th century
The Textile Museum, Washington, D.C.
Gift of Richard Ettinghausen

During the seventeenth century, India produced vast quantities of rugs. Many of these, with distinctive designs of single flowering shrubs or elaborate floral and trellis patterns, have always been recognized as products of weaving under the Moghul rulers. Indian court miniatures of this period in fact depict such rugs with the utmost precision.

Other rugs, based much more closely on Persian designs, have posed difficult questions of identification. This group of rugs has been called many things over the years, most recently Indo-Persian, suggesting that the problems have not been resolved. It is to be expected that Indian rugs should follow Persian ones closely because historians tell us that under the emperor Akbar, late in the sixteenth century, Persian carpets were imported into India and carpet weavers, undoubtedly Persian, settled in Agra, Lahore, and Fatehpur Sikri.

In spite of its very worn condition, the large fragment shown here still displays the grand and rich color scheme and the beautifully drawn and detailed compartment design which must have provided an extraordinary effect when the rug was new. The design consists of offset rows of multilobed compartments, each one defined by a scrolling vine in two colors, with little projecting growths and delicate tendrils winding around. The compartment scheme was shown in depictions of rugs in fifteenth-century Persian miniatures, and it developed into this very floral, elaborate curvilinear design in the late sixteenth- and seventeenth-century rugs produced in luxury materials in the Persian court manufactories—the so-called Polonaise rugs (see, for example, Dimand and Mailey 1973, nos. 19 a and b). Such rugs were frequently given as royal gifts to foreign dignitaries, ambassadors, and rulers, and may well have influenced Indian weavers; the rugs of Herat on the trade route between India and Persia may have borne similar designs. The border design in the fragment derives from a Persian model, perhaps the rugs produced in Herat. Large palmettes are framed by straplike reciprocal arabesque bands.

When it was acquired, this fragment was thought to be Persian, but the qualities which suggest an Indian rather than a Persian origin are the drawing, with an overdeveloped naturalism unfamiliar in heavily stylized Persian designs, and particularly the coloring, with its heavy use of oranges and light greens. The use of related colors side by side, here pink and red, is a popular convention in Indian rugs.

The design in this fragment is unusual among those of extant Indian rugs, but there are at least two related pieces, one in the Museu Calouste Gulbenkian in Lisbon (Inv. Nr. T63; Pope 1964–77, pl. 118lb), and one in East Berlin (Islamisches Museum, Inv. Nr. 99.315; Erdmann 1962, no. 90) which survives only in small pieces. Another fragment from the rug shown here has been pointed out to me by Charles Grant Ellis (American Art Association 1925, no. 14); it is a full-width strip which shows that the field design was originally two compartments wide.

Provenance: ex-collection Richard Ettinghausen.

Not previously published.

TECHNICAL DATA
Size: 133″ (338 cm.) × 65½″ (166 cm.).
Warp: white cotton, 4 Z-yarns S-plied, alternates moderately depressed.
Weft: beige cotton, 2 Z-yarns, 3 shots.
Pile: wool, 2 Z-yarns S-plied, asymmetrical knot open to the left, 12 horiz. x 12 vert. per in. (144 per sq. in./2232 per sq. dm.).
Sides: not original.
Ends: not original.
Colors (12): red, pink, orange, blue, green (3), yellow (gold), beige, dark brown, black, white.
Condition: extremely worn; areas of reknotting.

46.

KIRGHIZ RUG

Soviet Central Asia, early 19th century
The Textile Museum, Washington, D.C.
Gift of George Hewitt Myers, 1940

A small number of rugs have been generally associated with a nomadic people of Turkish origin called the Kirghiz. They occupy territory in Soviet Central Asia between Soviet and Chinese Turkestan. Hans Bidder records that the Kirghiz living south of Khotan brought their wool to that city to sell (1964, p. 37). Bogolyubov (1973, no. 51) illustrates a Kirghiz rug he attributes to the city or valley of Fergana.

The design of these Kirghiz rugs generally consists of a series of squares arranged in pairs with alternating group colors, each square bearing a floral or geometrized motif. The origin of these motifs has been the subject of some discussion. The rug shown here, a particularly appealing example of this rare type, has in each square a floral arrangement that seems to grow out of a single vase on a stand. Charles Grant Ellis (1967, no. 81) suggests that these compositions are based on misunderstood Chinese symbols—a pot on a teak stand, a halberd, and a jade musical stone forming the rebus "peace results in good fortune and happiness." A Chinese source is certainly possible, but it seems equally likely that this design element is a variant of the flowering shrub growing out of a vase seen in both Persian and Indian weavings.

The repeated composition in the present example is still clearly recognizable, but the blossoms and stems are beginning to take on a stylized quality. Other versions have much more schematic, stylized arrangements—either three vertical rows of angular devices or a main lozenge-shaped device with protruding "legs" at each end. Grote-Hasenbalg (1921, no. 106) illustrates a Kirghiz rug and relates the lozenge-shaped motifs to scorpions. All of these various elements seem to be more stylized versions of the design in our piece, suggesting that it may be an unusually early example.

Provenance: ex-collection George Hewitt Myers, who acquired the rug in 1914.

Published: Ellis 1967, no. 81 (not illustrated); Ellis 1968, p. 52 (left); Jones and Boucher 1973, no. 42.

TECHNICAL DATA

Size: 104″ (264 cm.) x 53″ (135 cm.).
Warp: mixed brown wool, 2 Z-yarns S-plied, warps even.
Weft: light brown wool, 2 Z-yarns S-plied (slight), 1 shot.
Pile: wool, 2 Z-yarns, asymmetrical knot open to the left, 7 horiz. x 9 vert. per in. (63 per sq. in./976 per sq. dm.).
Sides: red wool around 3 cables of 2 warps each.
Ends: plain weave at top, warp fringe.
Colors (9): red, pink, light orange, medium blue, dark blue, blue green, yellow, brown, white.
Condition: various small reknotted or patched areas; sides repaired.

47.

RUG WITH A POMEGRANATE DESIGN
Chinese Turkestan, late 18th or early 19th century
The Fine Arts Museums of San Francisco.
H. McCoy Jones Collection

One of the most ancient rug-producing areas in the world is Central Asia. Various sites around the Tarim Basin in Chinese Turkestan have yielded numerous pile-woven fragments dating primarily from the third and fourth centuries A.D. Many of these weavings differ structurally. Some have symmetrical knots; others, single-warp knots; and still others, asymmetrical knots with cut loops (reviewed with references by Eiland 1979, pp. 110–12, 230–33).

Several cities in the same area are known to have been rug-producing centers in more recent times. Kashgar, Yarkand, and Khotan, all oasis towns on the old Silk Route running south of the Tarim Basin, are mentioned by historians and travelers for their rugs (Bidder 1964, pp. 23–29), although evidence marshalled by Bidder suggests that Khotan was by far the most important. The extant eighteenth- and nineteenth-century rugs from Chinese Turkestan used to be called Samarkand rugs, probably because that was the source for Western merchants. Specialists have tried to identify certain types of rugs with the different sources on the basis of design or weave. Eiland (1979, p. 119) suggests that rugs with wool wefts may be from Khotan, but no specific attribution will be attempted here.

The rug illustrated here is a superb example of the Chinese Turkestan type. The field pattern consists of a single pomegranate bush growing out of a small vase at the bottom of the field. The pomegranates themselves form a pattern of diamonds in offset rows. A peculiar convention is used in depicting the pomegranates—the outer skin has been removed in order to display the proliferation of seeds inside, perhaps a reminder of the fertility symbolism of the fruit. Pomegranates have traditionally had this symbolic significance to the Chinese, but they favored depictions of the fruit alone. Cammann (1972, p. 53) thus argues a Persian origin for the pomegranate bush motif. The main border design consists of a row of unconnected eight-petaled rosettes, while the outer borders contain the continuous T-fret and swastika patterns that are popular in Chinese rugs.

Such rugs were made for use on the platforms that surround the central atrium of the oasis house. On smaller rugs this pomegranate pattern is shown once, and on larger rugs the pattern is shown four times (see Dimand and Mailey 1973, no. 231).

Provenance: ex-collections Michael Kalman, H. McCoy Jones (acquired rug in Egypt).

Published: Royal Ontario Museum, no. 41; Ellis 1960, no. 46; Ellis 1967, cat. no. 79, fig. 2; Ellis 1968, p. 50.

TECHNICAL DATA
Size: 98³/₄″ (251 cm.) x 50″ (127 cm.).
Warp: white cotton, 4 (some 3) Z-yarns S-plied, alternates moderately or strongly depressed.
Weft: mixed white and brown wool, single Z-yarn, 3 (sometimes 2) shots.
Pile: wool, 2 or 4 Z-yarns, asymmetrical knot open to the left, 8 horiz. x 7 vert. per in. (56 per sq. in./868 per sq. dm.).
Sides: red wool around 2 warps.
Ends: top has plain weave, knotted warp fringe (little remains): bottom has plain weave, warp loops.
Colors (6): red, pink, dark blue, medium blue, light yellow, dark brown.
Condition: sides, lower right corner, top left repaired or reknotted; a few small reknotted areas; red somewhat corroded.

48.

RUG WITH CLOUD-LATTICE DESIGN

Chinese Turkestan, 19th century
The Textile Museum, Washington, D.C.
Gift of Jerome and Mary Jane Straka

It is not surprising that rugs woven in oasis towns situated on the Silk Route should employ designs and motifs found in Chinese, Indian, Turkoman, and Persian rugs. Indian influences are most apparent in repeating designs of compartments containing single flowering plants or in trellis designs with elaborate scrolling vine patterns (see König 1975). The three-medallion arrangement so popular in these rugs is thought to derive from Buddhist sources, originally Indian (Bidder 1964, pp. 53–57). Turkoman influences are found in *gul*-like rosettes (Bidder 1964, pl. XIV). Persian influences are numerous; the *boteh*, the pomegranate bush (see no. 47), and several other repeating patterns are Persian in origin.

Chinese motifs are particularly prominent in this coarsely woven, but striking, rug. The field design consists of a "cloud lattice" in blue on a red ground. This element is seen in many East Turkestan pieces, in Kirghiz pieces, and particularly in Chinese pieces (Dimand and Mailey 1973, no. 199). The four-lobed medallions are derived from Chinese cloud motifs. The inner border is a stylized version of another cloud pattern (Bidder 1964, figs. 18, 19) or the Chinese wave pattern. The poorly centered reciprocal trefoils derive from cloud forms, and the continuous swastika designs in the guard bands are another element popular in Chinese weavings.

Provenance: ex-collection Jerome A. and Mary Jane Straka.

Published: Ellis 1967, no. 75 (not illustrated); Ellis 1968, p. 50 (right); Straka and Mackie 1978, no. 55.

TECHNICAL DATA
Size: 108¼" (275 cm.) x 70½" (179 cm.).
Warp: white cotton, 4, 5, and 6 Z-yarns S-plied, alternates slightly depressed.
Weft: white cotton, 3 Z-yarns, and brown wool, single 2 Z-yarn, used in random fashion; usually 3, occasionally 2 shots.
Pile: wool, 2 Z-yarns S-plied, asymmetrical knot open to the left, 7 horiz. x 5 vert. per in. (35 per sq. in./442 per sq. dm.).
Sides: not original.
Ends: warp fringe.
Colors (7): red, pink, medium blue, light blue, yellow, dark brown, white.
Condition: large number of small reknotted areas, particularly in the red field.

49

SMALL MEDALLION RUG
China, 18th century

Rug weaving is not one of the ancient arts of China. The vast majority of the Chinese rugs extant were produced in the nineteenth or twentieth century and are essentially commercial products, however pleasing they may be. Some remaining pieces may be as early as the reigns of emperors K'ang-hsi (1662–1722) or Ch'ien-lung (1736–1795). Rug weaving in China may well have begun in the interior provinces of Kansu or Ningsia, adjacent to the ancient rug-producing area of Chinese Turkestan. Both of these provinces, as well as the city of Ningsia, are situated on the Silk Route.

The small rug shown here is one of these early pieces. It was designed for use on the floor or on a *k'ang,* or couch, and illustrates aesthetic standards different from those evident in the products of the Islamic weavers. These are essentially the aesthetics found in textiles, translated into pile weavings. The clarity and spaciousness of the design are notable. The central roundel and the two flanking "pendants" are made up of sinuously coiling or writhing dragons, benevolent symbols in Chinese tradition which came to represent, in a particular form, the emperor. Corner pieces consist of brackets in a fret design, while the main border is a continuous swastika design.

The coloring of this rug is typical of Chinese pieces, with its emphasis on beige and blue. Only five colors are used, but certain subtle effects are still achieved— the two blues used together in the corner brackets or the dark brown and light blue or light brown circles forming the eyes of the dragons. There is disagreement among specialists as to the original coloring of these rugs. Ellis maintains (1967, pp. 4–5) that the Chinese were simply incompetent dyers who specialized in fugitive reds. In his view, the coloring would originally have included reds and other vivid colors much in the manner of East Turkestan rugs (see no. 48). Eiland, on the other hand, suggests (1979, pp. 25–26) that if the Chinese had intended to have vividly colored rugs, they had dyes at their disposal which would have successfully produced them.

This rug is one of a small group of pieces with similar design, coloring, and very coarse weave. One is in the Metropolitan Museum of Art (acc. no. 08.248.1; Dimand and Mailey 1973, no. 225), and another is in Hamburg (Museum für Kunst und Gewerbe, Inv. Nr. 1968.55; Hempel and Preysing 1970, no. 14).

Not previously published.

TECHNICAL DATA
Size: 55″ (140 cm.) x 28¹/₂″ (72.5 cm.).
Warp: white cotton, 4 Z-yarns S-plied, warps even.
Weft: white cotton, 4 Z-yarns, 2 shots.
Pile: wool, 4 Z-yarns, asymmetrical knot open to the left, 7 horiz. x 4 vert. per in. (28 per sq. in./434 per sq. dm.).
Sides: not original.
Ends: worn to pile.
Colors (5): light blue, dark blue, dark brown, light brown (may have been red), beige.
Condition: edges worn; overcasting on sides replaced.

50.
SADDLE COVER
China, 18th century
The Metropolitan Museum of Art, New York City.
Gift of Joseph V. McMullan

The Chinese wove large numbers of saddle covers in a wide variety of designs. Such pieces were placed over the hard saddle to cushion the rider (see Cammann 1972, p. 47, n. 21). The covers consist of two identical pieces, woven separately and joined at a central seam. The pile of each half leans away from the seam, a particularly practical arrangement that adds to the rider's comfort. Four holes pierce the fabric for anchoring; these are sometimes embellished with leather attachments.

Such saddle covers are often associated with Kansu Province and with the city of Ningsia. Joseph McMullan considered them Mongol products (1965, p. 371), Ningsia functioning as a marketplace for Mongol rugs, but some specialists consider the rugs products of Kansu (Lorentz 1972, pp. 136–37) or simply of northern China (Dimand and Mailey 1973, fig. 271).

Because these saddle covers were subjected to hard wear, most of the surviving pieces must date to the nineteenth century at best, but a few, such as the present example, may well have been made in the previous century. A broad variety of designs are seen on saddle covers, but most of them involve circular medallions or an all-over repeating diaper pattern. This example has a most unusual design known as the "cracked ice and plum blossom diaper," a design seen on porcelains produced during the reign of K'ang-hsi (1662–1722) and later. In the seemingly random pattern of triangles can be found a regular pattern of small rosettes. This is effectively framed by a border which typically consists of solid-color bands of varying widths.

Provenance: ex-collection Joseph V. McMullan.

Published: McMullan 1965, no. 137; Arts Council of Great Britain 1972, no. 137; Dimand and Mailey 1973, p. 310 and fig. 271.

TECHNICAL DATA (provided by Nobuko Kajitani)
Size: 58" (147 cm.) x 30" (76 cm.).
Warp: undyed cotton, 3 Z-yarns S-plied.
Weft: cotton, 2 Z-yarns combined.
Pile: wool, 2 (2 Z-yarns) S-plied, asymmetrical knot open to the left, 8 horiz. x 7 vert. per in. (56 per sq. in./868 per sq. dm.).
Sides: warps cut according to shape of piece, held by wefts; no added warps, no overcasting.
Ends: cut.
Colors (5): light blue, dark blue, light brown, medium brown, white.
Condition: considerable wear, especially on edges and center line; several reknotted areas; dark brown corroded.

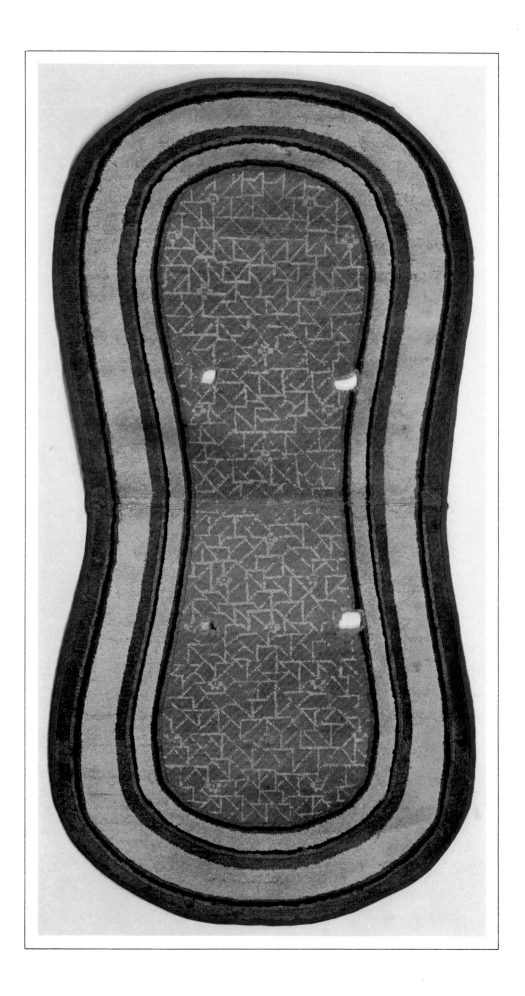

CREDITS

Excerpts from *The New Yorker* reprinted by permission; ©1939, 1967 The New Yorker Magazine, Inc.

Color photographs: nos. 29, 34, 47, courtesy of The Fine Arts Museums of San Francisco; no. 20, courtesy of the Fogg Art Museum; nos. 6, 13, 36, 50, courtesy of The Metropolitan Museum of Art; nos. 21, 23, 30, 40, 43, 44, 45, 46, 48, courtesy of The Textile Museum; nos. 7, 25 by Schopplein Studio, San Francisco. All others by Sotheby's Photographic Studios.